The St. Louis Woman's Exchange

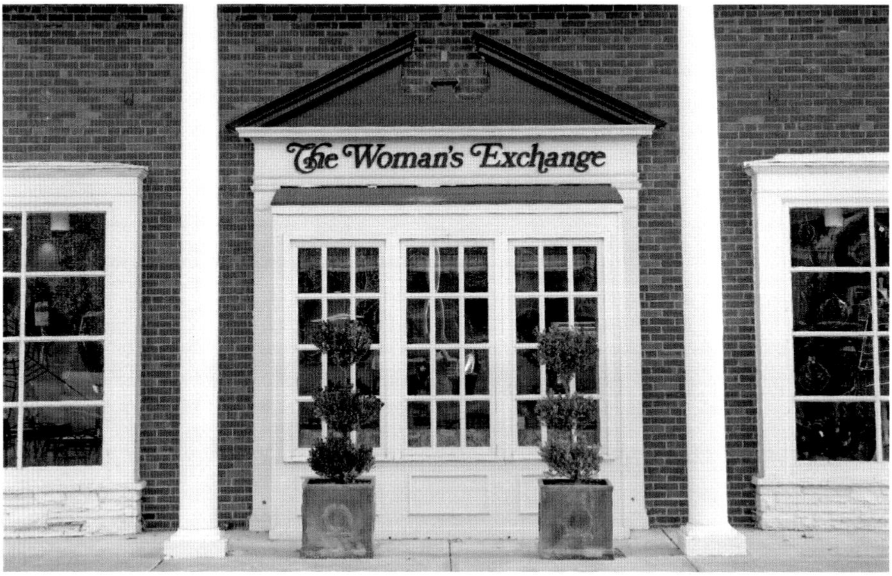
The Woman's Exchange

The St. Louis Woman's Exchange

130 Years of the Gentle Art of Survival

Jeannette Batz Cooperman

THE History PRESS

Published by The History Press
Charleston, SC 29403
www.historypress.net

Foreground cover image courtesy of Richard Benkof Photography.

First published 2012

Manufactured in the United States

ISBN 978.1.60949.113.0

Library of Congress Cataloging-in-Publication Data

Cooperman, Jeannette Batz, 1961-
The St. Louis Woman's Exchange : 130 years of the gentle art of survival / Jeannette Batz Cooperman.
p. cm.
Includes bibliographical references.
ISBN 978-1-60949-113-0
1. Woman's Exchange of St. Louis. 2. Specialty stores--Missouri--Saint Louis--History. 3. Markets--Missouri--Saint Louis--History. 4. Handicrafts--Selling--Missouri--Saint Louis--History. 5. Women artisans--Employment--Missouri--Saint Louis--History. 6. Women--Societies and clubs--Missouri--Saint Louis--History. 7. Nonprofit organizations--Missouri--Saint Louis--History. I. Title.
HF5429.5.S25C66 2012
381'.14--dc23
2011051272

To my mother, who taught me to appreciate fineness—in people as well as things.

Contents

Acknowledgements 9
Introduction 11

1. Stitched in Secret: 1832–1899 13
2. Hand in Glove: 1900–1929 37
3. Binding the Edges: 1930–1949 44
4. Eye of the Needle: 1950–1969 59
5. Classic Wins: 1970–1989 71
6. Cherry Picking: 1990–present 96

Conclusion. The Art of Preservation 121
Appendix A. Consignors 127
Appendix B. Staff 145
Bibliography 155
Index 157
About the Author 160

Acknowledgements

My warmest thanks to the staff, board members and past presidents of the Exchange, who scavenged for photographs, unearthed handwritten meeting minutes more than a century old (their original punctuation and spelling have been preserved) and searched their memories for the stories that made this book so much fun to write. Jacque Thieme made me tea and told me stories, Rindy FitzGibbon photo-styled still lifes of monkeys and bunnies with unfathomable patience, Kelly Hoerr organized and nudged, Nancy Thomas Xeroxed and brainstormed and Janey Rouse lent a hand every step of the way. Thanks also to the kind archivists in Scotland and to Esley Hamilton, the master preservationist in St. Louis County, for helping solve a few puzzles along the way. And above all, to the consignors, who opened up about past heartaches, struggles and self-doubt. Now there's the sweetness of knowing their work is treasured by strangers, passed down from one generation to the next. I wish we could all surround ourselves with such quality.

Introduction

On the surface, the Woman's Exchange of St. Louis is an exquisite gift shop with an adjacent tearoom—beloved, always packed, the chatter light and feminine, the salads and pies perfect. You're seated by an aproned woman who was probably photographed the night before in a sequined ball gown attending a charity gala. You assume that her smooth blond bob and pearls indicate a life of ease, private schools, country clubs and naïveté. She is stuck, by virtue of her tradition-bound upbringing, in a bygone era. Her life has been stitched together as delicately as a Victorian sampler, and she is cut from as fine a cloth.

So not true.

Oh, the facts might occasionally correspond—and the salads and pies are indeed perfect. But the volunteers who run the Woman's Exchange have had enough grit to keep the place going through two world wars, a Great Depression, several recessions, the end of fine craftsmanship and the start of a new DIY movement. They've made radical changes through the years—and have wisely known what should never change. The "decayed gentlewomen" they set out to help in 1883 are now refugees from Afghanistan, battered wives and mothers of sons paralyzed in Iraq. And while volunteers might occasionally don opera-length gloves (monogrammed at the Exchange, of course), they're just as quick to roll up their sleeves and paint chairs, scrub up a toddler's far-flung meal or tactfully furnish an apartment for a woman whose life has fallen apart. ("Could you possibly live with this sofa? I've been trying to find a home for it!")

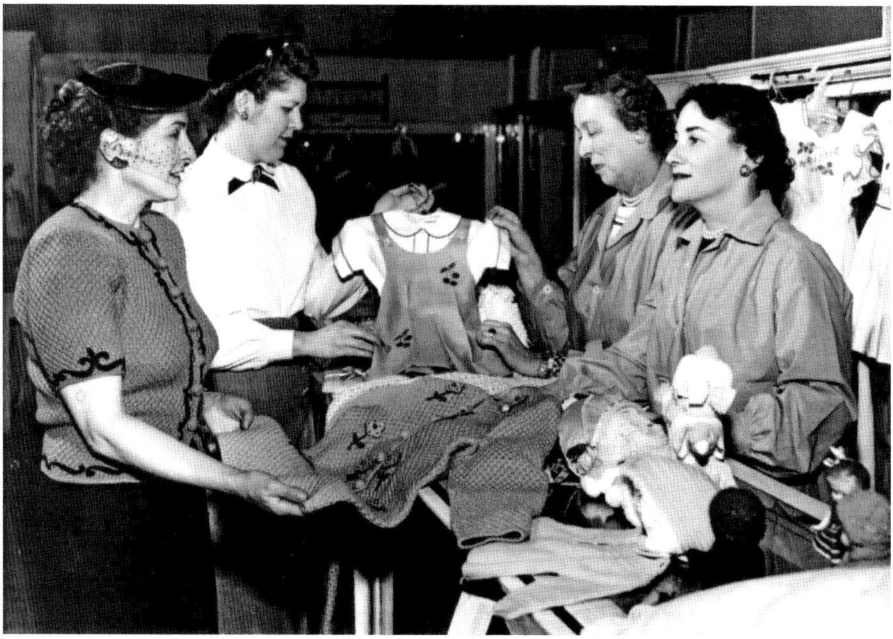

The woman at the far right is Ellie Shoenberg, a voice of conscience at the Exchange for decades.

Dozens of their counterparts in other cities have given up. The Woman's Exchange movement once spanned the country; now, only eighteen Exchanges remain. The St. Louis Exchange, 130 years old in 2013, is the largest left standing and its most thriving.

Credit usually goes to its founder, Ariadne Lawnin, for setting the right tone. Or to St. Louis itself, in many ways a southern, old money city, fond of its traditions and famous for its philanthropy. But in the end, it's the volunteers and the consignors who make the Exchange work. They exchange not just handwork and money but also experiences, kindnesses and opportunities. They work hard for one another, and they buy one another different kinds of freedom.

1

Stitched in Secret

1832–1899

Women came to the back door at nightfall, their pale faces hidden by veils or bonnets, and left soft bundles of finely embroidered baby dresses, pantalets and quilted petticoats, modesty pieces and knee warmers. The next morning, other women, clad in finer silks, chattered lightly as they unpacked and tagged the garments for display in the shop. As soon as they were sold, cash would travel, with the same swift secrecy, back to the seamstresses, so they could buy coal and food and clothe their own children.

It was a scalding shame for a well-bred woman to be penniless in the nineteenth century and even more mortifying to go out to work. Yet parents and husbands died, and a family's wealth could vanish in a day. "In no country in the world are private fortunes more precarious," wrote Alexis de Tocqueville after traveling the United States in 1831. "It is not uncommon for the same man in the course of his life to rise and sink again through all the grades that lead from opulence to poverty."

If a man's fortune was precarious, imagine the prospects for a woman without a man's protection. In Philadelphia, where this story begins, approximately 90 percent of the adults receiving relief between 1811 and 1829 were women.

Elizabeth Stott was not one of them. She came from a well-to-do Philadelphia family, and she'd married as well as everyone assumed she would. She threw lovely parties, showed her prize orchids and had her portrait painted. There was no expectation for her to do anything more.

But she wasn't blind to the world around her.

When she realized how harsh life could become even for a well-born woman, she invited sixteen female friends to her home. They were women like her: safely moored and anchored by family money, protected thus far from life's treachery but clear-eyed and compassionate—and perhaps a bit bored. Together they made what was, in their time, a bold and startling plan.

On February 1, 1832, Stott and her friends opened the door of the Philadelphia Ladies' Depository.

It was the first in what would grow into a nationwide collection of Woman's Exchanges. It was an unprecedented experiment. And it was successful almost immediately.

What inspired Elizabeth Stott? There are two accounts, both likely to be true. In the first, she is out shopping, and she watches from the corner of her eye as a young woman tries to sell a finely wrought piece of embroidery to the shopkeeper. He does not even pretend to negotiate with her, just brusquely offers a fraction of her asking price. Stott later learns that the woman is a widow trying to support four small children.

She might, of course, have gone to work at one of Philadelphia's garment factories. There, she would have been paid by the piece, so if she spent an entire sixteen-hour day making a fine linen shirt, she'd earn about seventy-five cents. For a woman in the nineteenth century, a factory job meant working long, exhausting hours in dimly lit, crowded rooms. She'd be exposed to contagious diseases and rough manners, and she'd be vulnerable to her boss's sexual advances.

She'd also be scorned as a failure, because women, by definition of their gender, had very specific duties. They gave themselves either to God or to man, and if the latter, their highest purpose was to bear children. Ministers preached that a woman's responsibilities lay in the home, and physicians warned that her reproductive organs would disintegrate if she did wage labor.

But what if she had no choice? In their first annual report, Stott and her friends declared their intent to spare penniless women "the dangers and humiliations associated with wage earning" and to shield them from "the rough and unkind treatment to which they are frequently exposed in their efforts to obtain employment."

Stott's other possible inspiration came a year before she opened the Depository. She went abroad, sailing by clipper ship to London and traveling north to Scotland. There, she wrote of seeing impoverished gentlewomen's handiwork sold for their benefit in a place called the Edinburgh Depository.

The Scottish archivists I consulted could find no official record of such a place. One gentleman triumphantly sent information about the Royal Edinburgh Repository and Self Aid Society, which fit the bill perfectly except that it was not founded until 1882. There was also a Royal Edinburgh Society for the Sale of Gentlewomen's Work, but the earliest committee minutes in the Staffordshire Archives only date to 1885.

Victoria Garrington, a researcher at the Museum Collections Centre in Edinburgh, dug deeper and found an 1839 reference to the already established practice of upper-class individuals selling items on others' behalf. "Waldie's Select Circulating Library mentions Lady Howard, who spent the Season in Moray Place and Charlotte Square, having a back room full of crafts by people who had fallen on hard times," she wrote me. "Perhaps what Elizabeth Stott saw was a private enterprise like this, a precursor of the 'official' societies?"

What matters now is that her recollection of the "Edinburgh Depository" lent shape to her generous impulse the following year. The Philadelphia Ladies' Depository set up shop, quite deliberately, in the fashionable Girard Row neighborhood their customers would frequent. Just one year later, the Depository had 225 dues-paying members and was the city's third-largest charity. An 1835 ledger sheet noted that consignors had made 197 custom shirts, 196 chemises, 64 nightgowns, 89 caps and 48 nightcaps, not to mention more than 248 yards of goffered (delicately crimped or fluted) lace that would have strained their eyes well into the night.

Two years later, the Panic of 1837 broke out, causing a financial hysteria that lasted well into 1840. A few members of the Depository were stunned to find themselves in distressed circumstances, forced to turn for help to the society they'd helped found.

PHILADELPHIA'S EXAMPLE INSPIRED A second exchange, the New Jersey Ladies' Depository, in 1856. Then the bloodshed of the Civil War began, and women left their cozy firesides and rolled up their sleeves to do volunteer work. After the war, they didn't go home. Instead, many joined the Woman's Christian Temperance Union and started shutting down saloons. This was housekeeping writ large: they'd decided it was up to them to clean up society's messiest problems. And they'd reached the giddying realization that, if they banded together, not much could stop them.

The national Woman's Exchange movement caught this energy. In 1878, Louisa May Alcott, author of *Little Women*, and Julia Ward Howe, author of "The Battle Hymn of the Republic," helped found the Boston Women's Educational and Industrial Union. That same year, the elegantly bohemian Candace Wheeler, one of the nation's first female interior and textile designers, decided this movement seemed perhaps a tad narrow and snobbish. Why help only "decayed gentlewomen"? She and her own group of friends formed the New York Exchange for Woman's Work so women of all classes would have an outlet to sell their work.

The following year, the Women's Christian Association in St. Louis opened an industrial sewing school and boardinghouse for young women. Funding was slow to come, though, and the scope felt limited. One of its volunteers, Ariadne Worthington, wanted to do more.

Ariadne was a remarkably down-to-earth society belle.

She was born in 1840 on a farm near Creve Coeur Lake. Her father's land was beautiful—a long, narrow strip of one hundred acres, rolling and wooded at the edges, extending south from the lake. (Creve Coeur Park's Greensfelder Shelter now sits where some of his crops grew.) But Albert Worthington died when Ariadne was three years old, leaving her mother, Elizabeth Sappington Worthington, alone in the country with two small children.

Elizabeth eventually gathered up Ariadne and her brother and moved to the city. Now, instead of cicadas and tree frogs, they heard clatter, yells, clopping hooves and ringing hammers. Hotels and factories were going up, a theater was opening and immigrants were streaming in from Ireland and Germany. St. Louis's river port was second only to New York's, and the Mississippi River was as crowded as a downtown street, with barges, steamboats, paddle-wheelers and canoes churning its muddy waters.

The Worthingtons moved into a respectable boardinghouse at 141 North Thirteenth Street, near what is now the Soldiers Memorial. From their doorway, they could look two blocks south and watch Christ Church Cathedral go up, stone by stone.

One of the boardinghouse's other tenants was Joseph DeMontalte Lawnin, a darkly handsome nineteen-year-old from Montreal. He'd been sent to Quebec to study for the priesthood. Weary of theology, he'd taught himself carpentry instead and then severed ties with his family and moved to the United States. Sailing downriver, he landed in St. Louis, where he established his own boatbuilding and lumber company.

And fell in love with the teenage Ariadne.

Five years later, on July 23, 1861, they were married. Ariadne was just shy of twenty-one, and Joseph, already called Captain Lawnin by the men on the river, was twenty-four.

An oval portrait—painted in oils and not terribly well—shows Ariadne with russet-brown hair and strong features, a squarish face and a hint of a smile. She's wearing an off-the-shoulder crimson dress and an ornate gold medallion. In her lap rests, oddly enough, a pumpkin. She is more stolid than lithe, and even with a gourd plopped down on her lap, she looks like someone who knows her own mind.

She bore Joseph two sons, Albert and Louis. Their father was soon well known as a steamboat joiner and cabin builder. He built the *S.C. Clubb* ferry; put the upper works on the *Annie*, the *Montana* and a new iron boat; and had a contract to build a side-wheel passenger steamer modeled after the *Golden Eagle*. It was sold before he finished work, so he sued. Meanwhile, he built $30,000 worth of icehouses on the edge of Creve Coeur Lake, near his wife's childhood home, because the area was thought likely to become a popular resort.

Ariadne didn't sit idle while her husband worked. She chaperoned young women to watch boat races on Creve Coeur Lake. She occupied a box at the opera with Joseph, who now styled himself "J.D. Lawnin." At an open house on Washington Avenue, she was reported as wearing a black velvet skirt with a white satin petticoat, flounced in white lace and caught up with a bunch of red roses and a fichu of oriental lace. She wasn't as frivolous as this public detailing makes her sound, though. In the Gilded Age, fashion was such an important signifier that women's attire, even at their friends' cozy card parties, was written up in the newspaper. Columnists made, straight-faced, such comments as the following, printed in the *St. Louis Post-Dispatch* on December 1, 1883: "There is not a lady in this city, whose eyes are not so dimmed with age as to be unable to see herself in the glass, who does not sigh for a handsome collar button."

Ariadne was put in charge of the Japanese Department for an International Tea Party to be held at the Pickwick Theater in February 1882. She traveled to San Francisco and then corresponded diligently with the Japanese consul there. She imported "Kioto ware" for the tea, along with quite a few other authentic Japanese decorative items. No sooner was the tea party over than she began helping plan the Armory Fête, persuading artists in the Sketch Club and a professor of history to help design her tableaux. She was to do the American tent, and her tableaux would open with Hiawatha's wedding and then move on to Plymouth Rock and the

Fountain of Youth, an allegory of the country's founding that featured a maiden in glistening crystal, all the hues of the rainbow on her head. It was all a splendid success, and the Chicago members of the Society of the Army of the Tennessee sent her a magnificent floral tribute.

More soberly, Ariadne also served on the board of the Women's Christian Association (WCA), formed in 1868 for the sake of young women who needed a safe place to board and a respectable way to earn a living. The WCA wanted to open a boardinghouse and training school, teaching dressmaking, plain sewing, mending, typewriting, stenography, telegraphy, bookkeeping, arithmetic and spelling, all free of charge. It made a start with a cooking class, then an industrial and sewing committee, and began selling women's handwork. Ariadne volunteered for the committee and helped the WCA raise money with a steamboat excursion (thanks, no doubt, to her husband's river connections). But the WCA couldn't raise enough money or interest, and as its larger project foundered, Ariadne and her friends grew impatient.

They wanted a project with enough scope to make a difference. They'd heard of the Woman's Exchanges in eastern cities, and after long, excited talks, they began amassing funds to open one in St. Louis. They would need, they decided, $1,000. Their first fundraiser, of course, was a riverboat excursion.

Just before sunset on Saturday, May 26, 1883, the steamer *Charles P. Chouteau* left the Washington Avenue wharf, reported the next morning's *Missouri Republican*, "and bore away, down stream, with as pretty as bevy [*sic*] of young ladies and as jolly a crew of young men as one would find in traveling from Dan to Beersheba."

The evening had, it would seem, only one flaw: two days later, several subscribers wrote a cranky letter to the editor of the *Post*, asking that planners of the upcoming St. George's excursion be told to "have every other dance a square dance—i.e., Lancers or quadrille, as more dance these dances than any others. The writer and a good many others were obliged to look on all the evening at the Woman's Exchange excursion, on account of the number of difficult dances danced."

Ariadne did like a challenge.

Next, she persuaded local merchants to donate silver, woodenware, graniteware, ironware, a stove, a stocked pantry and more cash. She and her friends came up with a crisp motto—"Helping Women to Help Themselves"—and a clear target: "the deserving poor." When a *Post* reporter asked just where this new Exchange would be, she told him, "You can say that it will be located on Sixth street, between Olive and Pine, opposite Thatcher's, after the 15th of September…We have leased the store next to the Messenger office on Sixth street, which was the best bargain we could get in that locality, and on the 1st of September we will begin fitting it up."

The new Exchange "will not sell to any but women," she added. "No men need apply." She did have a great many businessmen to thank, however. So on opening day, September 27, 1883, she invited them to a grand dinner (the fastest way to a man's heart). "Oyster soup, roast beef, venison, a number of entrees and salads, vegetables and ice-cream, cake, fruit, etc. were served by a staff of intelligent colored waiters," reported the *St. Louis Globe-Democrat*. Seeing the gusto with which their guests ate, the founders realized that men as paying dinner customers might not be such a bad idea. On October 2, the *Post* reported:

> *The ladies of the Woman's Exchange are working like Trojans for the success of the dinner given by them this week. They could accommodate a great many more guests every day, but still the patronage is very large. An impression prevails that the dinners are for women only. This is a mistake. They are given especially for the benefit of the dear creatures of the opposite sex, and there cannot be too many of them to satisfy the ladies.*

(This merry note was sandwiched between a piece on Jumbo—an automatic elephant, which, clad in a scarlet velvet robe, was going to flap his six-foot ears in an upcoming parade to advertise "Northern Pacific Railroad, Jumbo Line of the World"—and one on Miss Eva G. Meyers, the first lady clerk at the post office in eleven years. It had taken them more than a decade to get over her predecessor, who had married the assistant postmaster and abandoned her post.)

Women were just beginning to seek equal rights in society. Unfortunately, they still had a tendency to absorb, reflect and even perpetuate the stereotypes of their own gender. On October 5, the *Post* quoted one of the Exchange board members expressing her frustration with lady customers:

> *They come in here and buy a cup of coffee or some other little article that costs ten or fifteen cents, and on the strength of that occupy a whole table for an hour or two, and besides disarrange everything on it and make as much trouble for us as possible. Now the gentlemen come in, order a dinner, eat it, pay for it and leave. That is the kind of customers we like, but we will have only ladies after this week, and will have to part with our gentlemen customers.*

Another bit of discontent hit the paper on November 16. "Fault-Finder" wrote to the editor protesting the method by which consignors were selected. A woman's situation in life was put before a committee (only one member knowing her name), and they considered whether or not she was truly poor and deserving of help. "If it is thought she does not need to make money in this way, and can be sustained without labor, then her work is rejected," the writer noted. "If the committee desires to help those that help themselves, then let it take all work offered, for they know not the needs of the applicants."

A response was fired back the following day: "It is obviously impossible for the Exchange to undertake to sell everything that every woman wants to sell, and if the only fault to be found with the management is that found by 'Fault-Finder,' the management deserves to be congratulated."

The Exchange was already making a name for itself with small kindnesses, like donating meals to the city's newsboys in December. On December 16, three months after its opening, the Exchange held a grand Charity Ball at the Pickwick Theater. The purpose? To raise money to buy a new building.

At the ball, Ariadne and J.D. were joined by Pierre Chouteau and his date, Miss Nellie Maxon (eldest daughter of John Maxon of the Lindell Railway; she'd graduated the previous spring from the Normal School), as well as General and Mrs. Carr and other notable St. Louisans. They dined on raw and fried oysters, chicken croquettes, lobster salad, ice cream, wine jelly and Prince of Wales cake, while the Arsenal Band played on and $1,500 swelled the Exchange's accounts.

In the Gilded Age, form mattered as much as content. Social rules were spelled out carefully. The Veiled Prophet Ball regulations, for example, were published three months ahead of time. Men were to wear black suits with swallowtail coats and white ties, and seats were reserved for ladies until after the Grand Entrée of the Prophet (the reporter hinted at the summary removal of any man who dared rest his legs before then). Women's fashions were prescribed to the last detail: "The tan glove is au fait for fall dress," a *Post* fashion column announced, "although it must be the twelve-button length." Striped hose were over; the new color was electric blue. Fans were best in plain white silk with a small monogram; the huge variety of ornamental fans had made them seem a tad vulgar.

The tension of all this obligatory conformity was broken by little bursts of the irrational or the daring. People dutifully swallowed their cod liver oil and obeyed social codes with religious exactitude, but they also snuck off to séances and thrilled to news of Madame Blavatsky and her Theosophists. Young ladies began affecting the masculine in dress, wearing fitted waistcoats and tweedy Newmarket walking coats from England.

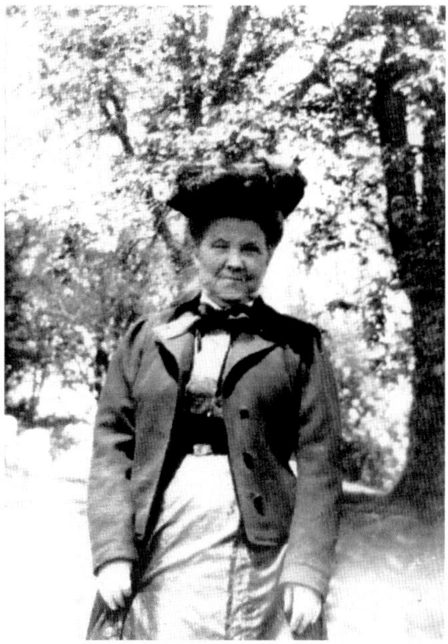

Mrs. Ariadne Lawnin, founder of the St. Louis Woman's Exchange.

Women were still held to be fragile, intellectually inferior and highly excitable, "swooning" at moments of stress. A headline the month the Exchange opened announced the "Arrival in America of a Hindoo Lady Who Will Study Medicine," as though it were heralding an unusual species.

The Exchange wanted women to be generally recognized as intelligent, competent and employable. In February 1884, after a newspaper article emphasized "the necessity of establishing some sort of charitable employment bureau, where worthy people may obtain honest work," Ariadne went straight to the mayor's office. She told him all worthy women applying for employment should be sent to her at the Exchange.

While much of its actual work was practical ("Gents' underwear neatly mended"), the Exchange's volunteers cherished lofty dreams. They spoke earnestly about giving women "a strong pull up the steep ascent of Life's hard, rough road." They urged one another forward: "Almost every one can bring in one neighbor and friend…Money we must have, to carry on this work."

They'd already found the 10 percent commission to be too great a burden on their consignors so had removed it (temporarily), making the St. Louis Woman's Exchange the only charity of its kind to charge nothing for services rendered.

The shop and lunchroom had initially opened at 214 North Sixth Street, but the new, more desirable location was 617 Locust. The Charity Ball's $1,500 in proceeds made a down payment on the $15,000 property. The next installment would be due in May 1884, so one of the board members, Mrs. W.L.B.G. Allen, wrote a play to be performed for the Exchange's

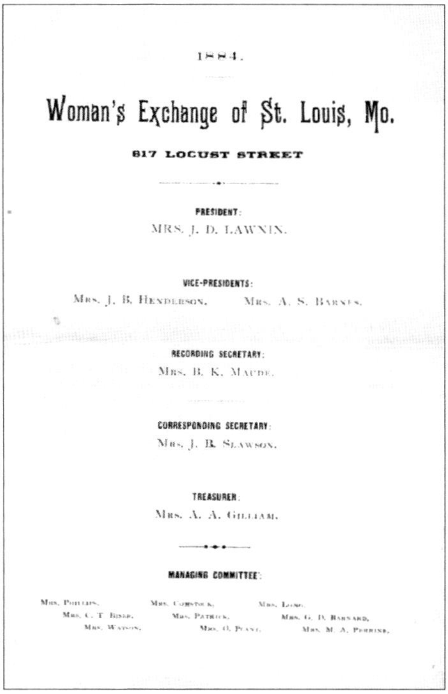

1884.

Woman's Exchange of St. Louis, Mo.

617 LOCUST STREET

PRESIDENT:

MRS. J. D. LAWNIN.

VICE-PRESIDENTS:

MRS. J. B. HENDERSON. MRS. A. S. BARNES.

RECORDING SECRETARY:

MRS. B. K. MAUDE.

CORRESPONDING SECRETARY:

MRS. J. B. SLAWSON.

TREASURER:

MRS. A. A. GILLIAM.

MANAGING COMMITTEE:

MRS. PHILLIPS, MRS. COMSTOCK, MRS. LONG,
MRS. C. T. [illegible], MRS. PATRICK, MRS. G. D. BARNARD,
MRS. WATSON, MRS. O. [illegible], MRS. M. A. PERRINE.

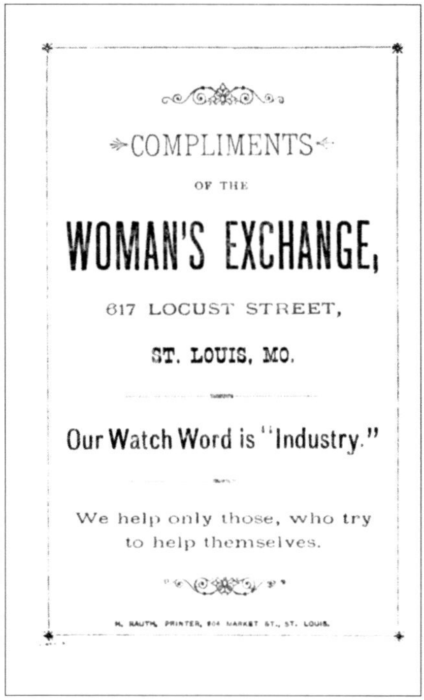

COMPLIMENTS

OF THE

WOMAN'S EXCHANGE,

617 LOCUST STREET,

ST. LOUIS, MO.

Our Watch Word is "Industry."

We help only those, who try to help themselves.

H. KAUTH, PRINTER, 804 MARKET ST., ST. LOUIS.

Above, left: Program for the 1884 meeting.

Above, right: Virtuous inspiration, compliments of the Woman's Exchange.

benefit at the Pickwick on May 13. Nine other board members pledged to collect $100 apiece, as did several donors, including liberal philanthropist N.O. Nelson, whose daughter would eventually marry Ariadne's son. The board felt entirely confident. It had been paying $2,000 a year in rent; now it would owe $3,000 a year for property that, in five years' time, it would own free and clear.

The Exchange moved into the Locust Building in April, and the board members breathed huge sighs of relief. There was so much more space! On the first floor, they'd have a large shop and an adjoining library and reading room, where workingwomen could improve their minds. There was also ample space for a lunchroom, where workingwomen, exhausted by hours gluing hatbands at the Bee Hat Factory, clerking at fancy shops, carefully inking the ledgers of annoying merchants who stank of tobacco or pounding newfangled typewriters could grab a quick pick-me-up—soup with bread and butter or a cup of coffee with bread and butter—for four cents. If they had a little more time and money, they could go upstairs to

THE WOMAN'S EXCHANGE
OF ST. LOUIS, MO.
SALES AND LUNCH ROOMS
617 LOCUST STREET.
Plain and Ornamental Needle Work, Darning, Mending, Chair Seating,
BREAD, CAKES, PRESERVES, JELLIES, &C.
Orders Received and Given for any Work that Women can do.
Lessons given in Embroidery, Art Pottery, Hammered Brass and Painting.
"We help those who try to help themselves."

A calling card for the Exchange listing its wares.

the workingwomen's dining room for something more substantial: "soup or coffee, bread and butter, one kind of meat, two of vegetables, and a dessert, for 16 cents."

The front dining room, meanwhile, would be reserved for ladies and, yes, gentlemen of leisure. Ariadne and her colleagues had changed their minds yet again, deciding it would be perfectly acceptable to serve men who were paying handsomely for their fare, as long as the inexpensive workaday lunches were restricted to women only. Judging by one day's sample menu, those in the front dining room could enjoy "roast turkey, quail on toast, baked trout, oysters in various styles, several kinds of pies and puddings, including plum pudding made by one of our consignors who is unrivaled by any one in the city."

Separating the dining rooms must have struck a few critics as elitist because the Exchange managers felt compelled to explain that the workingwomen needed a fast lunch, served upon arrival, and mixing the tables had caused confusion.

The Exchange settled happily into the grand Locust Building.

Within weeks, the building started to fall apart.

Extensive repairs and changes would be necessary, workmen informed the board, and these repairs could not be postponed. All the regular work of the Exchange would have to be suspended for four months.

The volunteers threw all their stymied energy into fundraising. In May 1884, eleven young ladies held a basket party, auctioning off festooned baskets to raise money to fill the library at the Exchange. Libraries were moral imperatives, and the literate made careful lists of what every home library should include, from the obligatory Bible, dictionary and encyclopedia to "good novels," which usually meant *Robinson Crusoe*, *Gulliver's Travels*, *Pilgrim's Progress* and *The Vicar of Wakefield*. But the young ladies were not entirely pale and serious; they persuaded the *Post* to write, "Handsome gentlemen are particularly requested to attend, as the girls want to have the nicest beaux that can be obtained."

Next, on July 25, 1884, the Exchange held a lawn party with music, dancing and an experienced palmist who sat deep in the leafy shadows, away from the moonlight and garden lights, and foretold brave guests' futures. Creative fundraising continued even after the shop reopened. On April 24, 1885, the Exchange held a grand children's fancy dress carnival at the Star Rink, and that June, another fundraising excursion sailed from the foot of Vine Street. "Prof. Jos. Kist will give an exhibition of high diving from the steamer while in motion," the *Post* promised. "He is a wonderful swimmer."

Even with the pause for renovations, the Exchange managed to serve more than fifteen thousand meals to "industrial women" and pay its consignors nearly $1,400 in its first year. In its second year, those totals quadrupled.

In January 1885, Ariadne found she could take time away from St. Louis to help set up the Missouri Women's Display at the World's Fair in New Orleans. She went with Mrs. J.B. Henderson, and a *Post* reporter followed them around as they began setting up. "We are going to insist on one thing at the start," Mrs. Henderson told him, "and that is, that our exhibit doesn't contain anything but examples of some useful female industry. We haven't a crazy-quilt or anything else that is crazy about the premises."

Ariadne chimed in, "Don't forget Silverine." The joint product of the ladies of the Woman's Exchange, Silverine was a whimsical substance "warranted to wash out the recollection of the past and furbish up a bartered old conscience into a semblance of shining silver." It was on display alongside a model house made of fireproof material, invented by Miss Nolan of Washington Avenue, and various other inventions. Less speculative artifacts included a miter, chasuble, stole and altarpiece, all embroidered and contributed by the Sisters of the Precious Blood. "Perhaps you didn't know that Missouri women are book-makers?" Ariadne asked the reporter, gesturing to a row of leather-bound volumes.

Mrs. Henderson added that once they'd filled their display case, they would "make ready a sort of bazaar for the sale of fancy articles for the benefit of the Woman's Exchange."

On the Fourth of July 1885, the *Post* printed "A Detailed Description of a Model Institution." The reporter described the Woman's Exchange windows' "magnificent" display of artwork. "So unpretentious, however, is the exterior that a large majority of persons either overlook it altogether or, from its quiet, changeless aspect, conclude that it is unoccupied," wrote F.E. Downes. "That quiet little store is sacred to that portion of humanity which mankind has universally agreed to call the 'better half.' It is the headquarters, the very essence of that explosive element in the make-up of society known as womanhood."

Indeed.

Downes speculated that the spirit of the Exchange must proceed from "the president, who is so enthusiastic in her work that it does one's heart good only to listen to her." He praised "that rare gift in woman, sound common sense, to which she adds a deep love of and sympathy for her own sex." A dozen women a day come seeking work, he reported. Older women are put to work in the kitchen and laundry, and "bright, rosy, trim little lassies" are taught to serve tables. "The woman who canes chairs there has a blind husband, a deformed boy and two babies," Downes wrote, quoting Ariadne's assurance that "this is the place where every working woman, girl and child may be sure of obtaining whatever sympathy and help she needs, no matter what her wants, no matter what her troubles." He no doubt mopped a tear as he wrote. But he ended with Ariadne in despair: "'But,' concluded the president, breaking off somewhat dramatically, 'I cannot act alone. When the public will not help, what can one lone woman do with all her theories?'"

Such melodrama wasn't like her, and the sense of helplessness her words conveyed was entirely out of character. As it turned out, she was exhausted. A week after Downes's article, the paper announced that Mrs. Lawnin would be taking a rest in Fort Reno with a lady friend because she was worn out from "her arduous duties connected with the management of the Woman's Exchange." Two weeks later, she inexplicably cancelled that trip. On August 1, she went to Mexico for a few weeks. On October 3, she was reported to be convalescing after a serious illness.

"A great many readers of the *Post-Dispatch* will be sorry to hear that Mrs. Lawnin, the indefatigable president of the Woman's Exchange, is very seriously ill," wrote the author of "Saturday Chat" on October 17:

> *Miscalculating her strength, she has toiled early and late, night and day, for the last two years in the interests of the charity which owes its existence mainly to her unwearied exertions. No work was too laborious or too menial for her to undertake, provided it was likely to enhance the prosperity of the institution, from presiding at the meetings to superintending the cooking for the V.P. Ball (the profits of which were handed over to the Exchange) and the almost entire superintendence of the excursions which were such a fertile source of profit this season to the charity. At the stand in the Exposition she was to be seen early and late until the severe attack of nervous prostration and low fever, from which she is now suffering, laid her low. The doctors are not at present very sanguine on the ground of Mrs. Lawnin's recovery, though it is hoped that her excellent constitution may effect a cure where a more delicate organization would succumb.*

Her constitution proved equal to the challenge, and she was socializing again by February 27, 1886. That evening, she won first prize at Mrs. Barnard's card party: a bisque shell mounted in silver, drawn by cupids and filled with flowers. It sounds god-awful, but at least she didn't win the booby prize: a box of candy vigilantly guarded by a china poodle.

The Exchange published its first newsletter, the *Mirror*, in December 1886. The lead article explained rather sharply that it was "not those who come to our doors in tattered clothing that we hope to assist, as they are an improvident class who have no appreciation of our motto 'Help Those Who Try to Help Themselves.'" (Note that the motto had already been tweaked slightly, however, inserting "try to" in acknowledgement of life's sometimes insurmountable obstacles.) "Nor is it for the sake of that woman's ware whose sphere in life, financially, will allow her to compete with capitalists," the newsletter continued, "but for those who daily walk beside us silently, unmurmuringly, their patient faces not disclosing the misfire they wage with life's misfortunes."

The *Missouri Republican* obliged with a little publicity, announcing that the new Exchange's consignors would be grateful "to obtain a mite" for their handiwork, and only moderate prices would be charged for lunch. For patrons interested in fine foodstuffs, the Exchange boasted cakes, jellies, preserves, mincemeat and plum pudding (old English), not to mention Neapolitan and nut cakes (made by Consignor No. 32), Parker House rolls and koumiss tonic. (A sweet, fermented milk drink, koumiss was said to ease digestive disturbances, respiratory problems and hangovers.) St. Louisans were urged to bring laces to be mended and chairs to be re-caned. A booklet described consignors' arasene (wool or silk used in working embroidery figures) and ribbon work, as well as paintings in oil and lustral (a method of painting over bronze). "Scholars are also desired in Repoussée," it added. And while younger women might dabble in the trendier crafts, "plain Sewing, Darning and Mending, Lace Washing and Kid Glove Cleaning are special features by which many old ladies, who have passed years of active usefulness, are making a support."

Consignors had strict rules to follow: "No perishable articles, such as Wax, Feather, Hair, or Card-board work will be received. No worsted goods, except ordered, will be received between May 1 and October 1. No preserved fruit received before September 1 or after April 1." The ladies were not about to store off-season goods, give the moths a summer meal, or risk food spoilage and bugs.

As for the volunteers who made up the board (every volunteer was a board member), they had to be nominated and approved to belong to the Exchange (still do). They also had to work for the Exchange at least thirty days a year or their resignations would be politely requested.

This was no frivolous endeavor.

Throughout the nineteenth century, the U.S. economy rose and fell, rose and fell. People slid easily from fortune to poverty—yet the distance between the extremes remained vast, without much of a middle class to bridge the difference. It was easy to become a homeless person, write Katharine Corbett and Howard Miller in *Saint Louis in the Gilded Age*, "because unskilled work was irregular and poorly paid, and employers routinely discriminated on the basis of race, age, and gender." In the mid-1880s, they note, William Tecumseh Sherman, Civil War general and real estate speculator, spent at least $15,000 a year keeping up his Garrison Avenue household. Bridget McHale, a widow with three children, was granted $5 a month in temporary relief.

Private charity was obviously crucial—but also something to beware of, the Exchange volunteers reminded one another. "Almsgiving without value received has annihilated the germs of energy and industry—two leading watchwords to success," noted the December 1886 newsletter. An article the following month made sure there was no misunderstanding: "The giving of alms to those who are able to work destroys their self-respect and lowers their moral tone until they become flabby—no bone in them—the frame of manhood is taken out and they cannot stand erect; they grovel in the dust, and have no delight in anything but that which is of the earth earthy."

The same writer was quick to cite examples of necessary charity: the Christian burial the Exchange gave "a poor weary woman worn out in the long struggle with poverty"; the job immediately found for her daughter; the tending of small children when their mother fell ill; the railroad pass purchased so a woman "in great need and distress" could reach her home in New York. But as a rule, the Exchange favored transactions that offered up hard work for fair recompense.

Nonetheless, a few critics wrote that this particular model of philanthropy actually did more harm than good, by selling the goods at low rates that then brought down the wages of workingwomen. Lucy Salmon, a Vassar College historian, criticized the Exchanges' anonymity policy, going so far as to say that by labeling consignors by number, it was allying itself with penal and reformatory institutions.

These were formal points for economists and social historians to debate. While they wrangled, the consignors were making money they desperately needed, and the volunteers were finding their own independence and learning the ways of the world.

They chose to emphasize cooperation rather than the competition they saw all around them. They studied their husbands', fathers' and brothers' methods carefully, though, and applied as many of these conventional business practices as they could. They knew they needed to win enough respect to hold their own in what was still very much a man's world.

Far from driving workingwomen's wages down, St. Louis's tiny Exchange soon became vulnerable to the garment industry and department stores. It survived only because its wares were unique, labor-intensive and entirely handmade. No assembly line could replicate Consignor No. 657's pen wipers or No. 36's pralines (labeled "very nice" in the inventory list), let alone No. 577's Spanish chowchow. No department store had access to such fine "Fascinators"—lacy, shawl-like head coverings in every possible shade—or such plush cases for opera glasses, hand sewn in rich tones of ruby, old gold, sapphire or emerald.

The Exchange schooled young women in common sense, virtue and "Good Society":

> *It is well to board conveniently near the church, so that in evenings and in bad weather, it may not be too burdensome to attend services. It is not wise to economize too closely about board. Try to be with good people, even if*

The Woman's Exchange Mirror.

Vol. I. ST. LOUIS, JANUARY, 1887. No. 2.

WOMAN'S EXCHANGE OFFICERS—1886-87.

President.
Mrs. W. B. Homer.

Vice-Presidents.

Mrs. J. D. Lawnin,	Mrs. S. D. Slawson,
" C. T. Biser,	" E. A. Clymer,
" Wm. Patrick,	" Mary Wetzel,
" M. A. Perinne,	" Geo. Taylor,
" W. B. Harris,	" Oscar Whitelaw,
" L. L. Culver,	" J. T. Watson.

Recording Secretary—Mrs. E. H. Long.

Corresponding Secretary—Mrs. N. O. Nelson.

Treasurer—Mrs. A. A. Gilliam.

Auditor—James E. Yeatman.

Legal Advisors.

S. Hermann,	W. B. Homer,
Judge J. H. McKeighan,	D. P. Dyer.

Advisory Committee.

Hugh Crawford,	I. N. Mason,
N. O. Nelson,	J. R. Lionberger,
I. G. Baker,	Geo. S. Edgell,
B. F. Hammet,	L. L. Culver.

Lunch Committee.

Mrs. E. A. Clymer, Ch'n,	Mrs. J. W. Gunn,
" Geo. Lynch,	" J. T. Watson,
" L. L. Ashbrook,	" Kain.

House Committee.

Mrs. S. S. Siever, Ch'n,	Mrs. J. D. Malin,
" L. L. Ashbrook,	" L. L. Culver.

Library Committee.

Miss Clare Gantt, Ch'n,	Mrs. P. G. Robert,
Mrs. I. Lionberger,	Miss Mary Sloan,
Miss Nina Matthews,	" Bryan,
" Emily Bryan,	" Bertha Drake,
" May Simon,	" Wilgus,

Mrs. L. Rogers, *Librarian*,
Miss Maud Reber, *Recording Secretary*.

A LETTER FROM OUR SECRETARY.

The question is often asked, "What good does the Woman's Exchange do?"

Although the work has been explained in our annual reports, and in various other ways, it seems to be of so much importance that it will bear repeating over and over again.

This institution, outside of its strictly legitimate work, accomplishes much good which is nearly lost sight of in the rush and turmoil of busy strife. Yet, doubtless the Recording Angel, who only notes the principle which prompts the heart to deeds of love and kindness, will be faithful to his trust.

Our work is constantly enlarging, and is purely benevolent. In all benevolent work there are great opportunities for good; but we must choose the wisest and best good.

Our charity does not cosist in almsgiving.

We do not wish to be classed with such institutions, for it would not be in accordance with our principle of helping those who are willing to help themselves; yet, there are those whom God in His providence has placed in such conditions that it would be impossible to help themselves. To such unfortunate ones, all hearts and hands should ever be ready with timely aid. Not long ago, a poor weary woman worn out in the long struggle with poverty, was given a Christian burial by the Woman's Exchange, otherwise she would have shared a pauper's grave. Her daughter was immediately given a situation at the Exchange.

Another poor woman with little children was very sick. The children were cared for at the Exchange several days,

The front page of the second edition of the *Mirror.*

> *it costs more…If good friends are hard to find, do not be satisfied with second-rate companions. Turn to books, and find recreation and inspiration in the best thoughts of the finest minds of all ages.*

The newsletter also gave wardrobe advice: "Nothing is nicer for the kitchen than calico," wrote Mrs. S.B. Kellogg. "It can be frequently washed; besides, it does not retain odors, as woolen does, reminding those who sit next to you of the cabbage and doughnuts you have lately eaten." She praised French saleswomen for dressing in black: "If one dresses in colors, there is apt to be confusion, unless one has money enough to have everything match, which is really very expensive." She tossed out one tip after another: "Avoid trimmings that become shabby before the garment is worn out…A good pair of black gloves is more ladylike than soiled light ones…The evils of tight dresses and thin shoes are well known, and a woman sins willfully if she wears them." In between the quick scoldings, she embraced her readers with expansive goodwill: "There is no good reason now why women who earn their living should not be among the best dressed women in the community."

The February 1887 newsletter waxed even more philosophical: "Your bank account is not your best treasure; it is what you are—what you have made yourself—what you have become." The same edition emphasized the Exchange's own ambitions: "We cherish the hope that at no distant date, we shall have canceled our financial obligations; and not until then can we, in any measure, reach the ideal of our work."

To that end, the Exchange held the Kirmess, or Dance of the Nations, in April. Modeled after galas back east, it featured international booths, costumes and rites—"not of to-day," the *Post* clarified, "but of a more picturesque and less practical past." Mrs. Adolphus Busch was in charge of the German booth, of course, and Tillie Orthwein performed in the Dutch dance. There were cowboys and cigarette girls in the American dance, a minuet from the French and a Mikado quadrille from the Japanese. The Russian box in the Music Hall was draped with furs, the German box in black and red, and a life-sized cow yielded milk at the Swiss booth. An invitation to the Kirmess, the Exchange's grandest fundraiser yet, was sent to Mrs. Grover Cleveland, the first lady, who declined.

Despite her absence, the Kirmess was hailed a brilliant success. A skirmish followed, though, when the ladies accused the *St. Louis Globe-Democrat* of misrepresenting their work, thanks to the malice of a reporter who had been refused admission to one of their planning meetings. The reporter's article hinted at friction between the workingwomen and the society ladies, claiming that factions had formed. This the ladies denied hotly, insisting there had never been a more harmonious project.

In any event, the event raised $5,811.

By now, Ariadne had turned over the presidency to Mrs. W.B. Homer and was taking it a little easier, hosting elegant "progressive euchre" parties (euchre was all the rage) and sailing to Europe with friends in July 1887. She was written up in the *Post* as an excellent cook, the chief example being her creative offering, at one party, of eggs à la militaire: boiled hard, peeled, rolled in raw egg and grated crackers and fried in hot lard.

Tastes change.

Her son Louis had graduated from Washington University with a mechanic's degree, and he was an enthusiastic player of lawn tennis. Her husband preferred entrepreneurship. In August 1888, he bought a three-story brick house on Lucas Avenue from Eliza Morgan for $4,000. He also had fun that month building a floating cage, so "poor children and gamins," as the *Post* called them, could swim safely in the river, which had become "a regular death trap for careless boys." The cage was suspended between two barges, and this improvised swimming pool was opened to both white and "colored" boys alike. They showed their appreciation with a great deal of enthusiastic yelling and splashing.

That fall, J.D. served on the elite Veiled Prophet committee, and Ariadne's presence was reported at several social events, once clad in lavender soie de France and on another occasion in mahogany faille. The Lawnins had "arrived"; Ariadne could have spent the rest of her days in elegant social pursuits. Instead, she kept her vision trained on the Exchange. By 1891, its finances were stable. It sold $3,632.35 in consigned goods that year and returned $3,273.67 to its consignors. Restaurant proceeds were more than triple the shop sales: $11,868—that figure included seventy-five thousand meals served to workingwomen—and the library issued 4,223 books.

Women's work was beginning to expand. On October 3, 1883, a *Post* article had noted that the average girl "can, if she is very lucky, secure a situation as a saleswoman in a dry goods or fancy store…She may, if she has a special training, become a milliner or dressmaker. Some women become excellent amannenses [*sic*]." Then, just eight years later, an article on June 7 noted that "the advertising departments of two of our largest houses are managed by ladies…The managing editor of one of the most prominent St. Louis weekly papers is Mrs. Maria Johnston…Recently a lady has filled a position at the Mercantile Library." That article went on to say, "There are a number of St. Louis women who are prominent in society who are in reduced circumstances, and who add to their income by beautiful fancy work. They take it to the Woman's Exchange, and it is sold without their names being made public."

On May 27, 1892, Mrs. E.H. Long, wife of the superintendent of public schools, was elected president of the Exchange. She was full of energy; a gifted musician, she had devoted her early years to study and practice, until a serious illness left her invalid for more than two years. When she recovered, she did not resume her music; instead, she affiliated herself with the Exchange and worked tirelessly for its cause.

Later, in 1892, someone at the Exchange had a brief but intriguing idea. Relations between households and their domestic help were deteriorating fast, with rancor and dissatisfaction on both sides. Something had to be done. What if the Exchange formed an Association of Housekeepers and Bureau of Information and acted as liaison? The goals, as outlined in the *Post* on June 5, 1892, were

> *to arrive at a more intelligent understanding of the means by which skilled labor may be secured and a respect cultivated for household labor; to promote a more scientific knowledge of what constitutes housekeeping and homemaking; of the economic value of food material and its nutritive conservation by good cooking and to consider and study all questions which concern the health, happiness and economic management of the family.*

The idea sounded earnest, noble and quite progressive—but judging by its absence in the minutes, it never got off the ground. Perhaps everybody was just too busy. On July 23, 1893, the *Post* reported that one consignor for the Exchange had made more than $1,000 that year just baking bread, and through the Exchange's employment bureau, eighty-eight girls had obtained situations. The five-cent working girl's lunch, served on china on a fresh white tablecloth, might consist of a bowl of gumbo, buttered bread and tea, coffee or milk to drink; for an extra five cents, a dessert of canned apricots or pears, prune pudding or lemon pie could be had. Granted, there were no finger bowls, but the women could wash up in the toilet room before returning to work, and if they had a few minutes to spare, they could relax in the reading room, browsing through books or conversing. (One afternoon, the topic was Buddhism.)

The reading room was all that was left of the library, which had closed early in 1893. St. Louisans had voted that the Public School Library Society, which stood only two squares away, be taken over by an independent board and opened, free, to the public. So the Exchange had added its own small but respectable collection to the new public library's ninety thousand volumes.

In May 1894, the women on the board found themselves torn over a proposal from E.C. Simmons to trade buildings. He was offering his residence, on Olive near Twenty-eighth Street, in exchange for their building on Locust. On May 6, a *Post* reporter wrote rather snidely, "If the opinion of one half about the other half were to be accepted the mooted question as to whether women may be trusted as financiers would be effectively answered." Two of the board members' husbands advocated the sale, but the Olive Street property was said to be not at all suited to the purposes of the Exchange.

On May 7, Simmons withdrew his proposition, saying there had been hints of disagreement among the ladies and suggestions that he was using a shrewd business trick to get the better of them, and he did not care to appear in that role. The board members informed him that they had decided unanimously to accept his offer, and had never doubted his good intentions; they'd only wanted to give themselves time to make a cool decision under consultation with levelheaded businessmen. They begged him to reconsider his withdrawal, but he did not.

That same year, the Exchange closed the Industrial Dining Room and the gentlemen's dining room, claiming both were draining them of time, money and energy. In lieu of the gentlemen's dining room, they began serving light noonday refreshments to ladies, relying heavily on their consignors' fancy foodstuffs and desserts. Then they turned all their energy to what they were calling the Business Woman's Dining Room. Members of the Exchange had founded the Business Woman's Club some years earlier, and it was thriving.

Life was changing fast for women; indeed, men were growing terrified. *The New Woman*, a stereograph now in the collection of the Missouri History Museum, showed a woman sitting with a newspaper splayed open, absorbed in reading, while her husband peers in from the kitchen, where he is wearily doing the dishes.

By 1895, the Locust Street building, bought for $15,000, was estimated to be worth $60,000. All around it, the city of St. Louis was booming. In 1860, the population had been 160,000; now it was over 600,000, making St. Louis the fourth-largest city in America. The dim yellow glow of gaslight was dispelled by harsh, bright white electric streetlights, and electric trolley cars were replacing the bumpy, mule-drawn streetcars that had left roughly twenty-three tons of manure on city streets every day.

People were nervously excited by all the progress but agitated by the social chaos that came with it: labor strikes, racial and ethnic tension, the anti-immigrant movement and, of course, "the Woman Question." What to do with them? Their proper place was the home and its immediate orbit: churches, schools, hospitals and private charities. But suddenly they had cash, thanks to Gilded Age industrialism, and they were meeting at tearooms, talking to businessmen, starting projects like the Woman's Exchange and shopping at big elegant department stores downtown.

Even though women were leaving the home more often, they chose its décor like museum curators. The industrial age had pushed the machine forward, and the decorative-arts movement wanted to restore the human touch. Victorians treasured the home as a refuge from all the buzzing, whirring confusion of the new era. Aesthetically, the timing was perfect for the Exchange: Victorian quilts were lavish, with satin, lace, brocade and velvet; Victorian garments were trimmed with lace and gewgaws; and Victorian decorating conventions created a demand for artwork and bric-a-brac. Even the simpler, more rustic decorative arts movement that followed—a deliberate counterweight to all that fuss—would renew people's appreciation for handcraft, fine textiles and needlework.

The Exchange had no shortage of work or customers; it only needed more volunteers. In the April 7, 1895 edition of the *Post*, Mrs. E.H. Long wrote:

> *We need more workers in order to increase the usefulness of this institution, and I cannot close this imperfect sketch without making an earnest appeal to the thoughtful women of this great city. It is almost impossible nowadays to avoid doing something for humanity's sake if we choose to, and yet there are those whose time is not their only capital who do not heed the cry of suffering women and children that are anxious and willing to make their own support.*

The Exchange was trying to shape morals, manners and aesthetics as well. The following year's December newsletter contained an article on "Taste in Wall Decorations," directing readers to "take it as a rule that dark colors are rich and light colors are pretty." Pastels were suggested for the boudoir; low tones of color for apartments of ceremony and state. "The hall may be treated entirely with Japanese leather in bronze, or a quiet olive tint, with rich frieze." The author added that the drawing room, "where the woodwork is either of cherry or mahogany, will be most pleasingly treated with old gold, or electric blue."

The same newsletter described two consignors' elaborate handcrafts:

> *A superb Barbotine vase, whose shaded blue ground gives a fair relief for the great clusters of cloth of gold, roses and buds that form its decorations, is a gem in ceramics, and will favorably compare with the foreign ware. This is the production of a young girl, known only as No. 139…A novel kind of sachet is also the work of 619, the covers made of fine linen, fringed and finished with drawn work at the ends, and the outside decorated with the name of the perfume within, etched in fancy letters in silks, suggestive of the flowers—as one of lavender, showing letters that grow like the stems of that herb, worked with lavender silk.*

How could those big, shiny new department stores compete with such detail? Granted, William Barr's emporium at Sixth and Olive had electric lighting, steam elevators, sumptuous dressing rooms and an exquisite tearoom—and in 1900, it would be bought by Hargadine, McKittrick Dry Goods Co., who would build the twenty-story Railway Exchange and give Barr's the first eight floors.

> *I was sitting by my scanty fire the night before Christmas. I had just one nickel in my pocket. My invalid son had gone to bed, and I was to awaken him early in the morning, that he might go and see if he could collect twenty-five cents that was due him for work, and as I was praying to my Heavenly Father for light, and asking Him not to let me starve on Christmas Day, a rap called me to the door, and there stood a messenger with a Christmas box from the Woman's Exchange. I was completely overcome, and felt that I stood in the very presence of God—He seemed to have come so near to me. I took it as a direct answer to my prayer, and I will not doubt Him anymore.*
>
> *—From an anonymous consignor, reprinted in the* Woman's Exchange Mirror *1, no. 3 (February 1887)*

The Woman's Exchange forged ahead, a tugboat surrounded by ocean liners. Quality mattered more every year. "It is unwise to send tawdry articles, and those devoid of all artistic effect," one member warned consignors, "as the large stores, with which we have to compete, are constantly filled with all that is beautiful; and unhappily, most purchasers do not supply themselves with novelties from principle."

The shop moved in 1898 to the corner of Tenth and Olive Streets and, in 1899, to North Grand near the elite enclave of Vandeventer Place—a location easily as fashionable as Philadelphia's Girard Row. By the century's end, seventy-two Woman's Exchanges had opened across the United States. The movement inspired Queen Olga of Greece to create a similar organization. The Contessa di Brazza of Italy—born Cora Slocomb in New Orleans—opened a lace-making school for needy Italian women that was inspired by her hometown's Exchange. Plans were underway for an Adelphi Association in Paris, which would find work for female members and sell linens, embroidery and other articles handmade by them.

So many people now knew of Woman's Exchanges that, in 1899, *Life* magazine published a cartoon in which a bemused, exasperated husband inquired, "Where did you say the Woman's Exchange was? I've something I'd like to swap."

2

Hand in Glove

1900–1929

On March 2, 1903, a Post *reporter wrote a colorful piece about a "Business Girl" cluing him in at the Woman's Exchange lunchroom. "'There is everything in putting on a shirtwaist right,' said the Business Girl, as a young woman came in whose pleasing figure had suffered none from absence of knowledge of shirtwaist effects. 'That's Miss Frances Feldkamp, a very bright girl, stenographer to President Hawes of the police board. The smaller lady with her in mannish costume is Miss Zulu Hudgens, public stenographer in the Lincoln Trust building, one of the most successful and brainy business girls in St. Louis…She is mannish only in dress.'"*

By 1905, the exuberant Teddy Roosevelt was president, Freud was writing boldly about sex and the first neon signs were decorating city streets. Ragtime's zany syncopation filled Tom Turpin's Rosebud Café. Scott Joplin had just left St. Louis, but he wrote "Rosebud" that year in homage to Turpin.

The Exchange was having a quieter celebration. That January, after the first board meeting of the year, the treasurer, Mrs. P.G. Robert, sat down, dipped her pen (fountain pens were not yet in vogue) and wrote neatly: "The last dollar of the amount borrowed to rebuild the back of the store has been paid."

"We feel it is due Mrs. Lawnin the Founder and First President to let her know how rich in blessings, and how wise were her counsels, and good her judgment, when she urged the buying of the property," Mrs. Robert continued. "There we followed her, but I do not believe one woman on the Board would have had the courage to lead."

They sent a basket of flowers to Ariadne's home, 4262 West Belle, and her most recent successor as president, Sarah W. Allen, wrote an accompanying note that was almost as flowery. She thanked Ariadne for helping them to "bear the 'burden and heat of the day' in the early life of the Woman's Exchange" and invited her to rejoice with them at the prosperity her courage had created. The building on Locust Street had steadily increased in value, and the income from its rental now secured their finances for the foreseeable future, "enabling the Board to greatly increase its usefulness." Sales were increasing just as steadily. They rose from $420.92 in November 1905 to $877.12 in November 1906.

Advice columnists now sent people to the St. Louis Exchange to secure hard-to-find articles, fine handiwork or merciful assistance. On June 27, 1908, a letter to the *Post* editor signed "Sympathetic" offered "suggestions for Mrs. A.," noting, "It is difficult to suggest ways of making money in the case of a wife with a number of children, especially if she is not strong. If she has any artistic skill, with needle or brush, she might try making a few fancy articles and putting them up for sale at the Woman's Exchange."

The board met monthly in one of the members' homes, beginning with the Lord's Prayer and ending with a light lunch or afternoon tea. Early reports were mainly about money and practical concerns, with committees reporting on "fancy work," "order work" and the "culinary department." Food sold especially well. In 1906, the Exchange had orders for one hundred fruitcakes, fifty plum puddings, chili sauce, tomato pickles and cream candy and desperately needed a good "salt-rising bread maker." Two years later, it was searching with equal vigor for "a good pound cake maker."

Word of the remarkable quality spread, and by 1907, the St. Louis Exchange was receiving orders from as far as Pasadena, California. Customers demanded more stuffed dates and fruit wafers, pecan and oatmeal wafers, sand tarts and molasses and spice cakes. Women bought many of the breads, pastries and canned foods they used to make at home. Fretting over the growing "servant problem" (immigration had leveled off, and there was no longer a ready supply of willing help), they purchased as much ready-made as possible and acquired machines to speed the remaining labor. First came sewing machines, then washing machines and then electric stoves and refrigerators. In 1909, the first commercial manufacture of Bakelite marked the beginning of the Plastic Age. Home and virtue were no longer synonymous; work and play in the larger world seemed far livelier.

In 1909, Ariadne, sixty-nine, lost her husband. She continued working for the Exchange for the next three years. In 1912, she agreed to move to Edwardsville to live with her son, Louis, and his family, and in 1915, she was paralyzed by a massive stroke. Two weeks later, she was dead.

By that time, her project was well established, and there were Woman's Exchange shops and lunchrooms in nearly every major city. Back in 1901, *Good Housekeeping* had published a list of all of them, and that list was still growing.

The push for suffrage acted like a good strong sniff of sal volatile, waking women's consciousness. A September 9, 1909 letter to the editor of the *Post* read:

> *He must be asleep if he does not know that woman is no longer considered a mere reproducing machine and that she is not now expected to sacrifice herself to the duty of adding to an already overcrowded world…The matrimonial bargain of today is ceasing to attract even the most eager bargain hunters. Only the men who benefit by it consider it a bargain at all.*

Similar ideals energized the board members of the Exchange, but they managed to keep a fine balance, fighting for better and more independent lives for women without alienating traditional views of domesticity.

They had too much practical work to do to lose ground fighting over abstractions.

In its first fifteen years, the Exchange had moved three times. Its members would stay restless for the next century, always searching for a better location or more space. In 1909, they found a white frame store and residence at Macklind Avenue and Arsenal Street, but their loan didn't go through. In 1911, they agreed to a ninety-nine-year lease for the property on Locust, locking in that rental income. In 1917, they moved to the corner of Maryland and Euclid in the Central West End.

That year, their "man," faithful Henry, who lifted heavy boxes, delivered packages and made repairs, died suddenly. At their next meeting, the saddened members moved to "investigate [the] condition of [his] widow" and make sure she would be able to manage on her own. That was, after all, their mission, and widows still had precious few options.

Even young brides had to get creative. In "Just a Wife (Her Diary)," reproduced in the *Post* in September 1916, a young woman detailed her hunt for viable employment:

> *I went to a woman's exchange. I saw wonderful, intricate fancy work, which must have taken hours and hours: costly embroidery that would cost me my eyesight. When I shook my head in despair the woman in charge asked me if I could do plain sewing. "Of course," said I, "you know I make all the children's things." Then she showed me hemming as fine as embroidery, and I realized that my knowledge of needlework isn't commercially viable. Preserves and jellies sold well, she said; but where could I get the raw fruit? I'm not a farmer's wife…Suddenly I realized the trouble with me. I was trained for nothing.*

In November 1918, after the cloud of the First World War lifted, the board borrowed $15,000 to triumphantly pay off the mortgage on 617 Locust. Mrs. L.F. (Lottie) Sexton, acting secretary, worded the report very carefully—"that the above and forgoing meeting was called and held in accordance with the by-laws of said corporation and the forgoing is a true and correct copy of the minutes of said meeting"—et cetera. The Exchange was determined to be businesslike; also shrewd. It now had five years to pay off the principal note, at a favorable rate of interest. Profits seemed likely. Mrs. Sexton's minutes noted a "great increase in our sales despite depressing influence of The War."

A fire started in the Exchange building in February 1919, its flames melting fixtures, scarring furniture and licking at the metal of the cherished Protectograph check writer. Much of the consignors' handwork was destroyed. Later, meeting minutes noted that, to the president's great relief, "the Insurance Company had made a very fair settlement."

That spring, "Mrs. Lovett reported that she has orders every Saturday for not less than twenty-five cakes, and they are increasing—also she has new charge customers and they are increasing. She suggests that we have a helper in the salesroom with a small salary as we have so many customers at one time, it is hard to give satisfactory service." Sales rose in the fancy work department, and in June, there was "a good report on hemstitching gowns and table linens, also a good sale of Bed Spreads."

The consignors grew assertive, asking that their accounts be paid faster. Abashed, the board members agreed. They also, however, raised the out-of-town consignors' commission from 10 percent to 15 percent. None objected.

A sugar shortage that fall made the hot demand for cakes impossible to fulfill. The board began adding special ready-made items to help defray operating costs. This was a radical move, given the Exchange's ethos, and

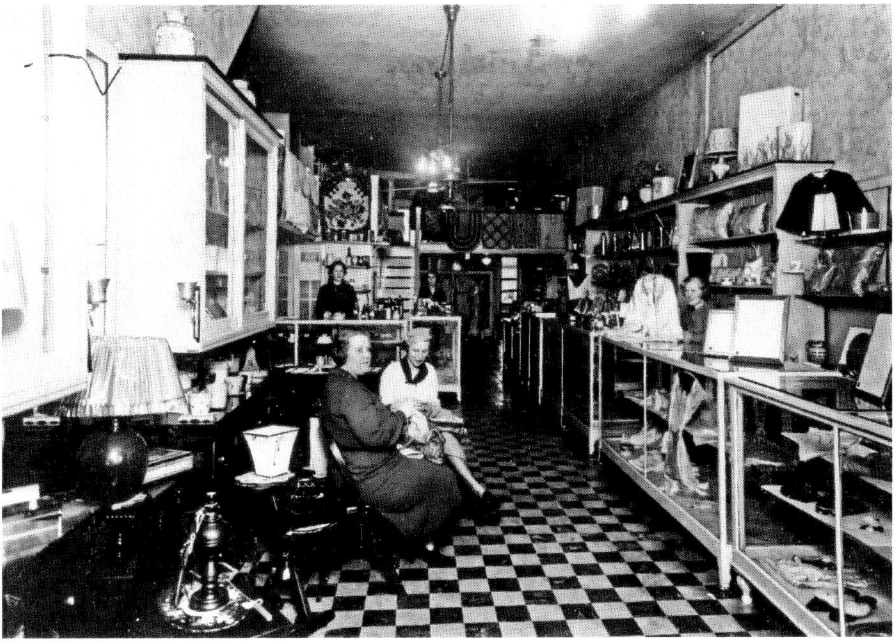

An early shot of the Exchange's shop interior.

fiercely resented by some. But the world had changed overnight; nearly everything was mass-produced. If the shop was to compete, the ready-made advocates argued, it would have to insert a few economies of scale. Besides, the "bought outright" items might attract shoppers who could be shown the more finely made consignor goods.

The decision was delayed, but the point had been made. For most of its future, the shop would carry a judicious mix of consigned and "bought outright" goods.

In 1920, women won the right to vote.

In 1921, board members eyed vacant space in their building, envisioning a baby shop or tearoom. They broached the possibility to their landlord, Mr. F.A. Banister, and learned that he was about to raise their rent for their current shop. Eyebrows arched. Mr. Banister held firm but suggested the ladies allow him to put an addition on the west, next to Mrs. Scullins's shop. "Together with that and the new building, we could rent it for the same amount we are now paying $160.00 a month," the secretary wrote. "It was decided if we could see the plans and have a voice in them, that we will agree to same."

Mr. Banister didn't listen closely enough, however—and the board members were not fools. By March, Mrs. Byrne had made a motion "that we give up anything Mr. Banister has to offer, as his rents are too high."

Meanwhile, the Exchange had found a man to replace Henry, a porter named A. Patrick, and he was proving invaluable. "Moved and seconded that Patrick's salary be raised $5.00 a month," the minutes read. "Moved and seconded that a rain coat be purchased for Patrick."

In 1922, the Exchange borrowed money again. It owed $2,900.00 in mounting bills and debts, not to mention $1,600.00 left from a loan taken out in 1920. Financial realities didn't sober the members, though; the '20s were too resolutely lighthearted. "Picnic luncheon orders taken," the Exchange advertised gaily. And indeed, by 1924 there was enough money to invest $3,119.27 in three Liberty Bonds, bearing a solid 4.25 percent interest and maturing in 1932. Salaries in 1924 ranged from $80.00 a month for Patrick, with a $5.00 Christmas bonus, to $125.00 for Miss Skipwith, the shop manager, who received a more lavish bonus of $15.00.

The controversy over "bought outright" items boiled over again in 1925. The Exchange had made a brief rule not to buy ready-made articles because the practice had triggered such fuss during the sugar shortage. Now a motion was made to amend that rule for pre-holiday items—subject to the board's approval, of course. (In 1929, frustrated by the tug-of-war, a member would go to the New York Exchange and inquire about its policy. "They too found it necessary to carry a supply of things bought outright," she reported triumphantly, "in order to draw customers for the consignors' products.")

The 1925 opening of a tearoom at 390 North Euclid offered a welcome distraction from the bought-outright dilemma. Tearooms were hot in the '20s, with alcohol verboten and women motoring all over the countryside in search of mild adventure. Trendsetters ranged from the bohemian Liberal Club in Greenwich Village to roadside teahouses in rustic New England and on the California coast. Run by educated, upper-class women, they were genteel and delightfully themey, lighthearted in atmosphere. Their crustless, triangular sandwiches, fancy salads and buttery pastries seemed innocent and sophisticated at once. And in St. Louis, the tearoom was a welcome relief, for the ladies at least, from country roadhouses with their big Anheuser-Busch signs and hearty German fare.

The Exchange tearoom would have serious competition to the east, though, in downtown St. Louis. Vandervoort's tearoom had already established several specialties, the most talked-about its frozen cream-cheese fruit salad. Stix, Baer & Fuller was famous for a seafood plate with toasted anchovy rolls. Nevertheless, the Euclid tearoom did splendidly, developing a recipe for chicken salad (on toast; in those days, everything nice was on toast) that remains beloved to this day. Customers made the tearoom a social rite, the younger women daring to arrive in their cloches and flapper dresses. (Not the fringy above-the-knee versions, though; those they saved for parties soaked in bathtub gin and the Charleston contest in front of city hall.)

In 1928, as the roar of the '20s grew faint, bakery revenues dropped sharply, finishing $1,072.50 lower than in 1927. That was the only hint of economic difficulty until September 16, 1929, when members found a discrepancy of roughly $2,000.00 in the books. "This cannot be satisfactorily accounted for as the old system of bookkeeping was so inadequate," the minutes noted, and you can almost hear the sigh. Luckily, the October 21 meeting recorded "a net profit of $306.72 for the month of September," higher than the previous September. Members' minds quickly turned to other issues: Mrs. Witherspoon had asked their permission to place her caps in the Exchange.

Three days later, on October 24, 1929, the market crashed.

There is no reference to the panic in the Exchange's calmly composed minutes. Black Tuesday passed without comment. Indeed, the report on December 16 noted "a net profit for the month of November of $491.71."

The work continued.

3

Binding the Edges

1930–1949

The 1930s were a more sober decade, grimly hopeful. Women dined at the tearoom in fitted, short-sleeved print dresses with thin belts and a long row of tiny buttons, wearing hats and gloves and sensible shoes and looking like the wives of Anglican clergymen. At night, the fur coats came out, often a bit ratty by now, along with the high heels. But there was a hint of Tennessee Williams's Glass Menagerie *in the prevailing mood. The forced gaiety was gone, capitalism had failed and families were stressed to breaking points.*

Depression notwithstanding, 1930 started with net profits in the spring, followed by a quiet summer. In fall, though, anxiety rippled through the shop. "It was felt that the children's dresses are not attractive," the secretary noted, and a committee swiftly formed to address the issue. Its members' surnames are recognizable in St. Louis to this day: Conant (Mrs. S.D.), Shepley (Mrs. E.A.) and Shapleigh (Lois). They did their job like executives called in to rescue a failing company. By the following September, the minutes acknowledged that "the Children's department had greatly improved."

Dismal sales of a November exhibit of hook rugs were the direst news until April 1931, when the calm was broken by a robbery. The booty? Lingerie, valued at about $125. The Exchange felt unable to pay the consignor for the entire loss but did reimburse her for the materials. Members conferred, trying to decide whether they should compel all new consignors to carry insurance themselves. For a shop as serene and orderly as theirs, there seemed an uncommon number of fires, floods and thefts.

In May 1931, the Exchange made its largest profit in more than a year. Members planned a joint fashion show with the Junior League and looked into the idea of "broadcasting on the radio-station K.W.K. at $30 an hour with a 13 week contract." One wonders what they would have broadcast for an hour at a time—sewing lessons? At any rate, it is unclear whether they signed the contract. Often, new ideas were broached by enthusiastic young board members and then researched more carefully or dismissed as profligate by the elder members. This was especially true in the austere '30s. Soon, instead of lavish advertising expenditures, they were pushing "the White Elephants," urging customers to come in to buy and to bring their own castoffs for sale.

From the January 15, 1934 meeting, there's an intriguing note: "The Board also decided that they did not wish to have Mrs. Worthington working in the Exchange or Tea Room—but that for the present she could use her psycograph machine on the balcony."

One wonders just what, precisely, Mrs. Worthington was doing. A psycograph was a phrenology machine, designed in the fervent belief that the bumps on one's head actually mapped one's character. The first psychograph was patented in 1905 by Henry Lavery. Alas, it had 1,900 parts and failed to work. A quarter century later, he was still perfecting his machine, which he wound up selling as a novelty for department stores and theater lobbies. Clearly, Mrs. Worthington believed in its value. And as Worthington was the maiden name of the Exchange's founder, she might have been a blood relation, commanding enough influence to hold sway on the balcony as long as she liked.

While Mrs. Worthington was measuring the skull bumps of ladies who lunched, the Federation of Woman's Exchanges was organizing nationwide. By 2001, when St. Louis's Sharon Bean became president, the St. Louis Exchange would be the third oldest in the organization, with the largest sales volume in the country. But in 1934, the big decisions were to buy a case for negligees, which were quite popular (remember the theft?), but not splurge on an electric sign for the tearoom, "on account of the expense."

As for the White Elephants, they didn't sell. A herd of them went to the basement, and their donors had to be begged to retrieve them to make room for storage.

In spring 1935, the Exchange decided to have a big sale of all its old stock, both "bought outright" and "as many consignor things as possible." It now had about 350 artisans submitting gifts, clothing and food. "Some consignors make quite a bit of money," the secretary noted in the January 1937 minutes, "so we really are helping them in a considerable way."

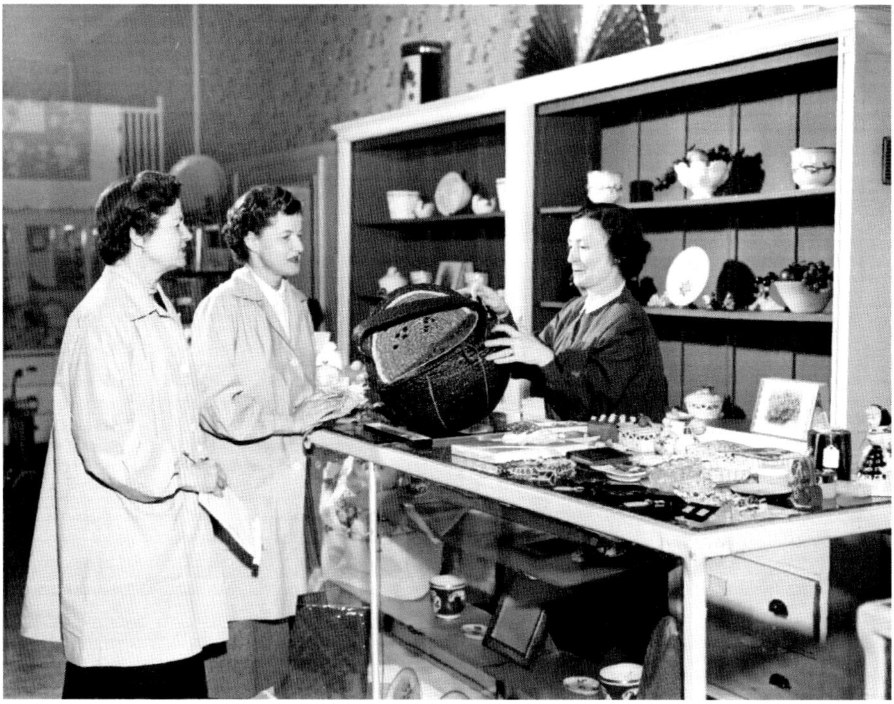

A volunteer shows off a watermelon basket sure to sell quickly.

Irene Dobler was now the manager. She'd given up a trip to Europe, she gaily told the *St. Louis Star Times*, to take over the reins in 1926. A horsewoman and a hyperkinetic volunteer, she was married to "a commission dry goods man" named George Dobler. She'd organized the local Food Administration office during World War I and served on boards all over town. Now she had the Exchange's seamstresses busy making ruffled bedroom curtains and slipcovers, organizing closets and dressing rooms (long before organizing closets became a trend) and going into people's homes to do their mending and darning.

Mrs. Dobler was a force of nature. She had a keen sense of competition and sent board members out to various shops to report on prices, lest the Exchange undersell or oversell similar goods. She watched money like a hawk. In 1937, as prices started to creep higher, she purchased extra tearoom supplies to store for future use. She did not stint on necessities, however. She urged a bigger coffee urn for the tearoom and a new commercial toaster for all those toast-point tea sandwiches. She resolutely ignored the new Fiestaware just coming into production, but she did agree "to try a machine that would type the menus for the Tea Room to save the girls time." She also had a pay phone installed, as the regular phone was being used too often by chatty customers.

In October 1938, board members talked eagerly about opening a tearoom in Clayton and then decided against it. The idea would return again and again, but each time it seemed too large an undertaking. Sales were down, but that could be rationalized. The previous year's profit had been unusual. Besides, the board noted, "the Tea Room continues to keep up, so that on the whole the Exchange did fairly well. It is thought that the Flynn Shop has affected business somewhat." Overall, the children's and fancy departments were down, and the bakery was up. Food was the nation's consolation after the lean years of the Depression.

At a special meeting called in February 1939, "Mrs. Vesper reported that a group of Jewish women were considering forming an exchange in Clayton to make money for the Jewish refugees. It was discussed whether it would be advisable for us to have a branch in Clayton going in a shop with

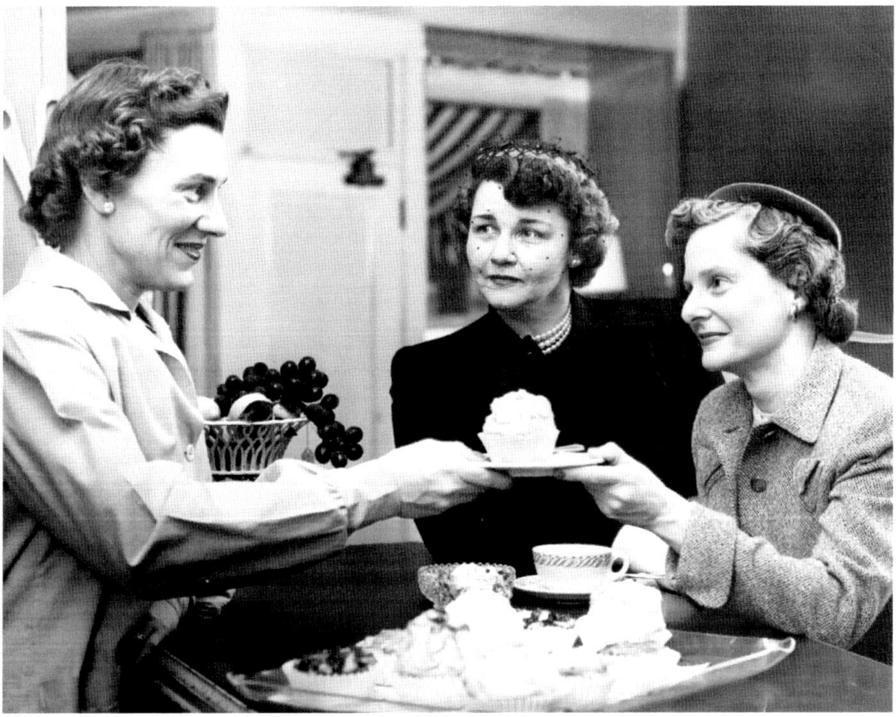

Jane Culver, offering a cupcake to two of her comrades.

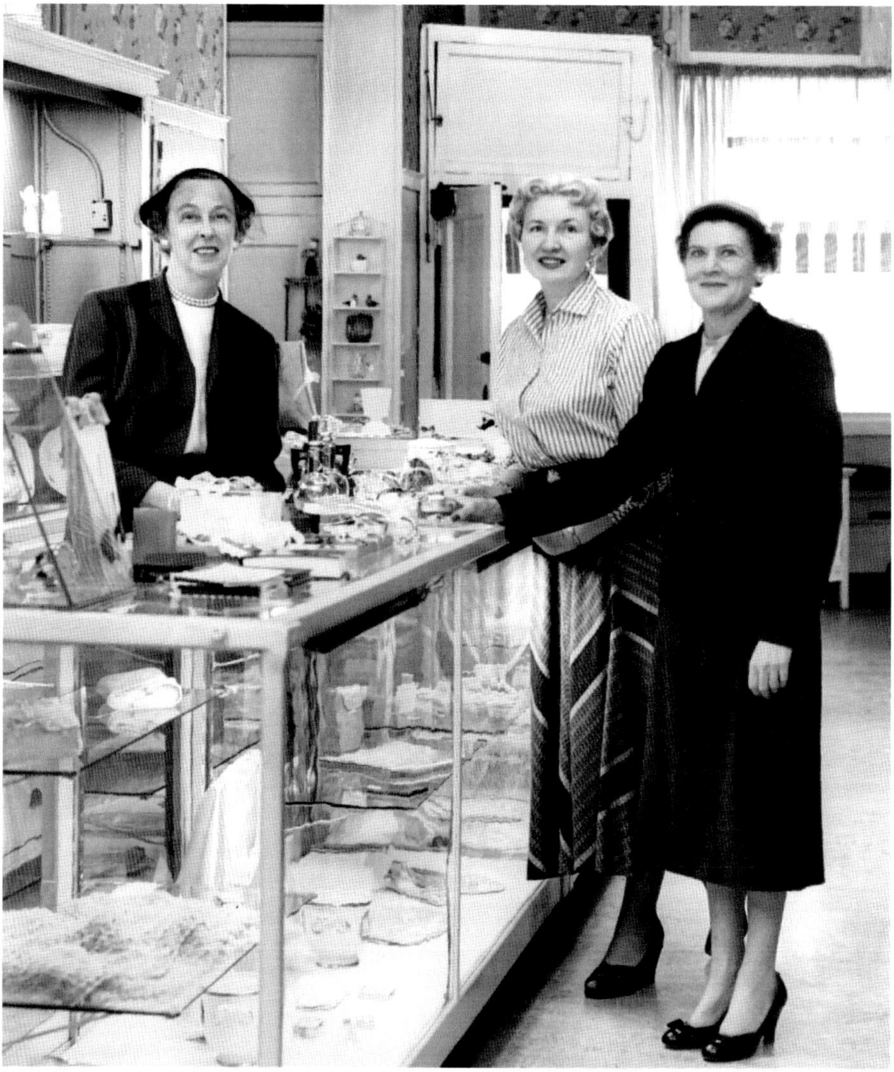

Exchange volunteers pose by a case of exquisite bridal and baby gifts.

somebody else." Later that month, a Realtor from Edward L. Bakewell Real Estate Co. came to a board meeting to discuss the advisability of opening a shop in Clayton. "She brought picture drawings of some of the buildings that have been erected and others that will be," note the minutes. Clayton had yet to build its sleek office towers, but it was emerging as a hot spot for retail and restaurants.

Sadly, the board abandoned the Clayton project once more. Instead, members decided to make the best of their current location. They would consult with a professional window-fixture designer to make the display windows more attractive.

So much for best-laid plans. The next month, they reported that "apparently there is no such person as an expert window designer in St. Louis." They decided to look into a grill made of wood as a window frame, instead of a grill of silver chromium, curtains and linoleum, which would cost $401.05. Next they discussed a new cooling system, but that would cost $1,700 for the tearoom alone. "It was moved and seconded that we do not put the cooling system in at present."

The board was thrifty but generous: "Pat, the janitor, has been sick with heart trouble," the secretary wrote, "and as we have had him 20 years, it was moved and seconded to give him $50.00 a month till other arrangements can be made." He died that summer. "The Exchange was

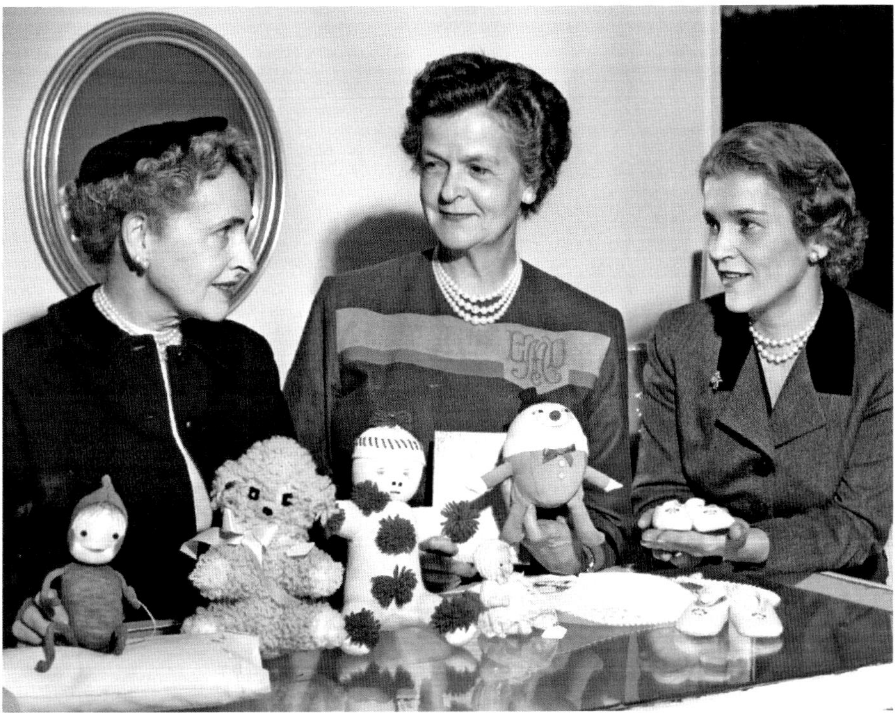

Margaret Archer (left), Carolyn McDonald (center; note her monogram, typical of work done at the Exchange) and Libby Culver (right).

able to help make him as comfortable as possible during his illness," the secretary noted gladly.

Around this time, Edie Spink, who later became mayor of Ladue and president of the Exchange, was a teenager at Mary Institute. She remembers going to the Exchange on Saturday afternoons after ice-skating at Forest Park. "We'd go for ice cream. For thirty-five cents you could get some cold bouillon and a sandwich and a drink and ice cream, but if you wanted chocolate sauce, it cost five cents more," she says. "In the summer, we'd go for lunch, eat, oh, probably a hamburger, maybe a chicken sandwich. We didn't eat salad in those days. The Exchange was on Euclid near Hortense Place, and sometimes it had fashion shows; people would come and model from the Ladue Shop or the fur shop."

It was all very glamorous, elegant, proper and, beneath the niceties, earnest in its mission. The Depression hadn't deterred the Exchange, and neither would the coming war.

At the start of the 1940s, war raged overseas, but all was calm in the tearoom. As it turned out, that air-conditioning the board members had decided to stint on had to be installed anyway, as a condition of their lease renewal. It cost $3,000, but the renovations won them some needed upstairs storage spacc.

In 1941, Mrs. Dobler suggested carrying a collection of linens from Madeira and opening the tearoom on Thursday evenings during the holidays, "so we can draw the men into the Exchange." (Interesting the husbands was always a special push at holiday time; they had gifts to buy for their wives, after all.) That fall, a Mr. Malloy from Bon Vivant went hat in hand to the ladies of the Exchange to tell them he wanted to open a restaurant and bar in his shop and serve lunches, dinners and drinks. He hoped they would not object. Mrs. Shepley and Mrs. Hotchkiss made a motion not to oppose his plan, and it carried almost unanimously—with only the formidable Mrs. Dobler dissenting.

America entered the war on December 7, 1941, and the bloodshed in Europe was uppermost in every adult's mind. In February 1942, the board deputized Mrs. Dobler to write St. Louis mayor William Becker to see if he would ask the people of St. Louis to pray for peace one minute each noon. Business continued steadily through the war years, with "a marked increase in receipts" by 1943: $43,566 higher than the previous year. A motion passed to invest $5,000 in government bonds. Mrs. Dobler was authorized to sign all ration point checks.

Mrs. Dobler's vigor may have been wearing on everyone's nerves, though. In January 1944, "it was decided to look for someone who might be able to work into Mrs. Dobler's position, in case she felt she would have to leave the Exchange at some later date." In February, "it was also decided to ask Mrs. Bransford Hill to come to the Exchange in April and work in as Mrs. Dobler's assistant."

She did so—and Mrs. Dobler continued on, as vigorous as ever.

By 1945, life had normalized. The postwar mood was high-energy, and women looked smart and determined in their tailored, shoulder-padded suits, with their hair rolled back smoothly and their lipstick bright. The lure of the new appliances had taken hold; the Exchange board members looked into an electric dishwasher, decided it was too expensive and wound up buying one second-hand. They were still yearning for some sort of "sound conditioning," to cut down on the clinking of cups and plates in the busy tearoom and a balcony over the Children's Department where bookkeeping could be done, freeing more display space. The minutes also note an urgent need "for consignors to make underwear."

Consignment sales rose the following year, as did tearoom sales, but the board remained thrifty: "It was suggested that we have music in the Tea Room but decided we could not afford it." The idea of a shop in Clayton was killed off definitively in 1946—again, out of frugality. Even the smallest crisis could dent the Exchange budget. In 1947, after much discussion, "a letter from the Service Bureau was received stating they will pay for one half the price of the long mirror on the door upstairs that was broken by one of their secretaries who in the meantime has left town."

Members wanted to be careful stewards of their funds but without appearing stingy. In 1947, they debated increasing the portions served in the tearoom. Mrs. Dobler warned that if they did, they would have to raise the price of the food. "It was decided we would leave it up to our patrons and place a questionnaire on each table asking them if they were satisfied," the minutes noted, "and if not would they like larger portions at an increase in price." Any psychologically savvy economist could have predicted the results: "It was unanimous that the customers were satisfied with the portions and prices."

By then, the Exchange had gone one better than Mr. Malloy and opened its own bar. After all, the New York Exchange had opened the Crinoline Bar back in 1934, and it had become famous almost instantly for its martinis and Manhattans. It had taken the St. Louis Exchange a solid decade—and some hot arguments—to follow New York's lead. One member quipped, "I came on this board with a prayer"—meetings were always opened with a prayer—"and I'm leaving with a cocktail lounge!"

Julia Lawnin Gordon—Ariadne's granddaughter, fondly called "Juge"—became the bartender. And even members who'd tsk-tsked over the notion of alcohol because they were convinced women did not, and should not, drink were persuaded to sip an old-fashioned on occasion.

Gordon's daughter was another Julia (today, her married name is Martin). She grew up on Westmoreland Place, just two blocks from the Exchange, and lunched there with her mother when she was a girl in the early '40s. "I had my velvet dress made there, with a lace collar, when I was seven," she recalls. "At nineteen, I went to Europe with Dian Chandler and [Carol Moon] Moody Gardner, who was Veiled Prophet Queen in 1949. The Exchange seamstresses made clothes out of nylon for us, so they wouldn't wrinkle, and we could rinse them out and hang them in our room. You couldn't go to a store and buy nylon clothes then."

Dian Chandler's mother, Tudie Chandler, was president of the Exchange. "She lived there, practically," recalls her daughter, now Dian Schock. "After my father died, that was her succor."

Dian loved wearing her white gloves to the Exchange for lunch with her mother. "The balcony was always very special; it was fun to sit up there." As she got older, she noticed all sorts of things. "There were two Friedas, waitresses," she chuckles. "One was little, one was big, and it turned out that Big Frieda was strapping steaks to her legs and stealing the place blind! Oh, and the volunteers wore very pretty aprons, like tulle, striped, with a bow in the back, and carried drinks to the tables. They had a great discussion about how to carry the drink without spilling it. 'If you look at the drink, you might spill it, but if you don't look at the drink, it's much more likely to arrive at the table.' Of course, none of these women had ever done anything like that!

"It used to be almost all consigned merchandise," she adds, "but during the war, a lot of the consignors got jobs in the factories." The best stayed, though—women like Jess McReynolds, who made several of Dian's debut dresses. "She was a marvelous woman. Very businesslike, a little brusque. Always had on a dusty rose smock with her measuring tape around her neck. My mother said that every year she wrote a letter to the board thanking them for the opportunity to sew for the Exchange. She was widowed early, and this was the way she earned her living—and sent her child through college."

Another miracle consignor began sewing in 1947: Violette Heim. She would hand-embroider nursery rhyme dresses for half a century, becoming one of the most famous and beloved consignors. When she began, she was either nineteen or twenty-two, widowed without warning when her young husband was shot and killed and with two small children to support. She lived in Highland, Illinois. Working in cramped quarters, stealing time whenever the kids napped or went to bed, she taught herself to draft patterns, cut fabric, stamp on the storybook pattern, embroider it and finish each dress with French seams. She made hundreds: Jack and the Beanstalk, Sleeping Beauty, Snow White, Goldilocks, Alice in Wonderland, the Pied Piper, the Wizard of Oz. Little did she know in those early years that someday three of her dresses would be worn by three sisters presenting flowers to the queen of England.

By 1949, the Exchange had reached a turning point. Board members were seeing a continuing monthly deficit and realized they had to use more caution in buying. Shoplifting in the Central West End was a huge problem, and they begged reporters at the city's three newspapers to write articles about it. They also found a merchandising manager from Vandervoort's, a friend of friends, who agreed to come to the Exchange and review its stock with Mrs. Dobler, board chairman Katy Lou Wade and Tudie Chandler. He went through the merchandise piece by piece, taking hours to scrutinize and assess the entire inventory. He told the women they weren't turning over their stock quickly enough. Hold an immediate sale, he urged, and then do some inexpensive redecorating and rearranging, put in some new lines of merchandise and discontinue some others.

"He spent quite a good deal of time going over the ready-to-wear stock," Wade reported to the board, "some of which he felt was much too old and should be moved at any price."

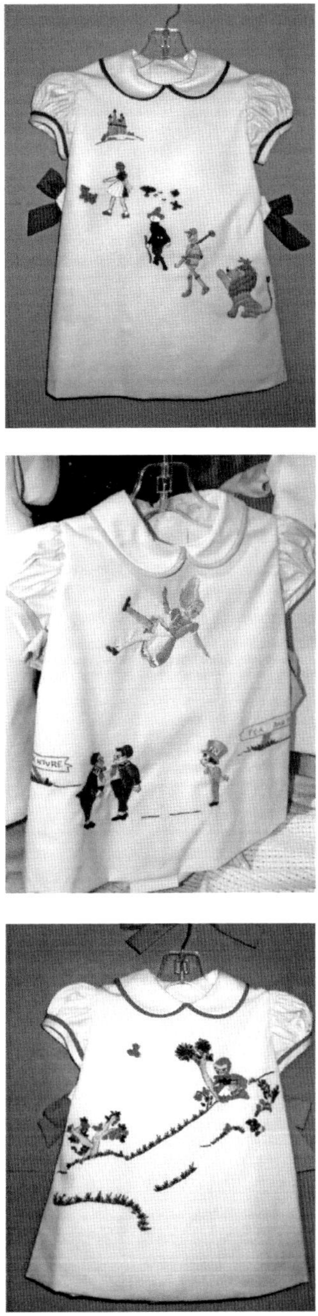

Violette Heim's embroidered fairy tale dresses

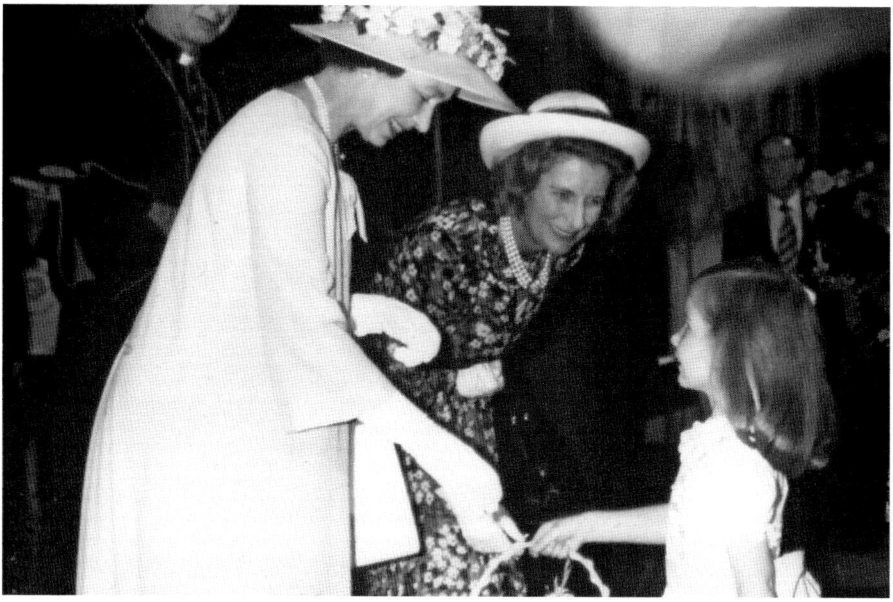

A little girl in a fairy tale dress presenting a basket of flowers to the queen of England.

He also pointed out that the coat-and-suit line they carried, "while a very good inexpensive line," could be found in Vandervoort's basement, and they should be handling merchandise of a slightly higher quality.

"He was quite impressed with a good deal of the consigned stock," she continued, "especially the baby clothes. He said that if possible we could enlarge that department and for 'bought out right' stock, perhaps buy some more baby things." He also suggested handmade underwear and negligees. "The rest of the consigned things he did not discuss in detail as of course that is our problem and the reason for the store." Ready-to-wear was the man's specialty, so he asked his store's silver, glassware and gift buyer, a Mrs. Merchand, to come the next day. She repeated his verdict: have a sale, take drastic reductions and get rid of the slow-moving stock they had been accumulating for a number of years. "Most stuff should be cut in half and the real junk cut about two-thirds or more," Wade reported. "She also made the comment that I thought was interesting, that all small stores should decide what price range they wanted to be in—the inexpensive which spilled over into the medium, or the expensive which spilled back into the medium, but not to try to have very expensive and very cheap stuff together as that wouldn't attract the same type customer and you wouldn't be known for one or the other."

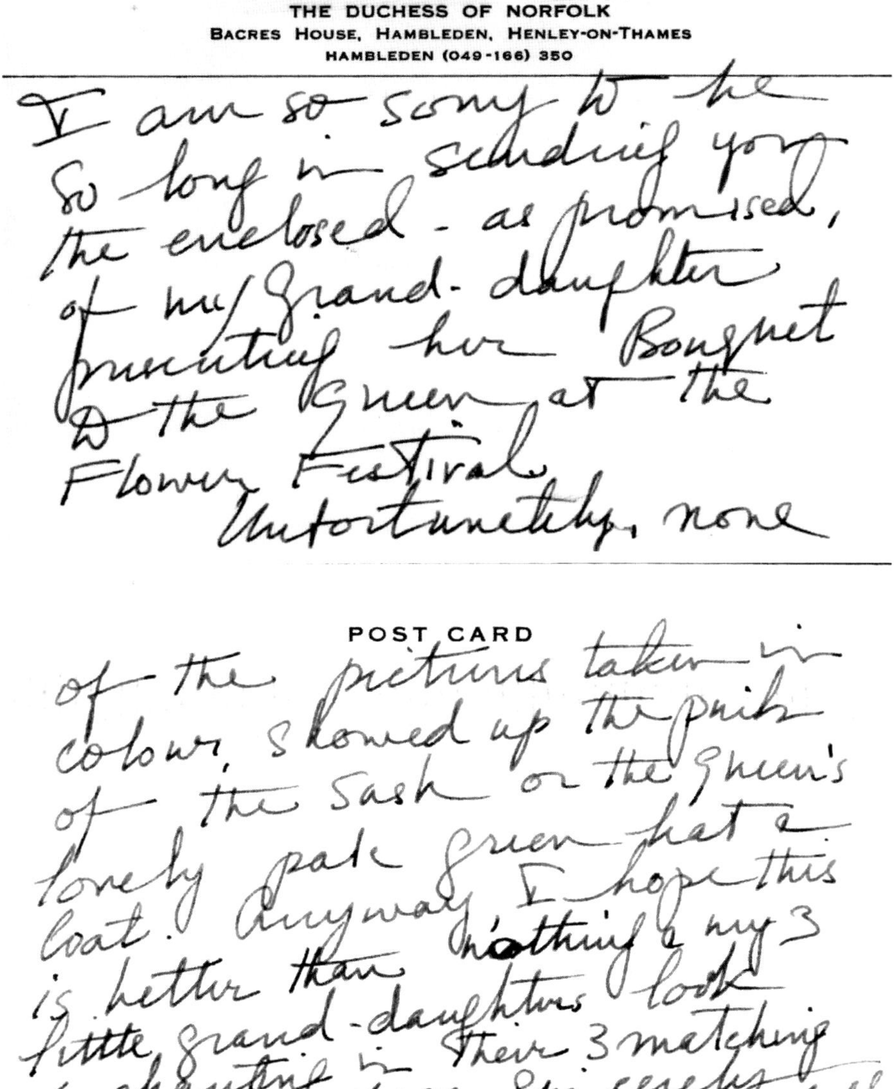

THE DUCHESS OF NORFOLK
BACRES HOUSE, HAMBLEDEN, HENLEY-ON-THAMES
HAMBLEDEN (049-166) 350

I am so sorry to be so long in sending you the enclosed - as promised, of my grand-daughter presenting her Bouquet to the Queen at the Flower Festival.
Unfortunately, none

POST CARD

of the pictures taken in colour, showed up the pink of the sash or the Queen's lovely pale green hat & coat. Anyway, I hope this is better than nothing & my 3 little grand-daughters look enchanting in their 3 matching dresses. Yours sincerely Anne Norfolk

A note sent to the Exchange with photos of the three sisters who met the queen in their matching dresses. The girls' grandmother apologized that the photos didn't properly show the pink of the dresses' lovely sashes or the pale green of the queen's coat and hat.

The board took the department store experts' advice to heart—which was easy, since that year's auditor's report showed a net loss of $5,603. When they began to emerge from the financial crisis, Katy Lou Wade handwrote a heartfelt letter:

> *Last spring when we has* [sic] *our reorganization, I found myself in the position of hiring myself as manager, in as much as I was chairman of the board at that time. I did this for the reason that I figured I had had some experience in running a small business, and the situation was so complicated that it would be hard to find just the right professional person to take it on at that point. Now that in spite of many ups and downs we are on a far evener keel and we know where we are and what the potentialities of the Exchange are, I feel it is only fittin* [sic] *to offer my resignation at this meeting. If the Board, after thinking it over from all angles, wish to rehire me I will be glad to consider going on with the job, or if they and you decide some one else would do a better job, I will be equally glad.*

The members emphatically assured Wade that they wanted her to stay.

By then, some of the kitchen staff had grown nervous about the future of the Exchange. Wade met with them and reassured them that the Exchange would continue on an even better scale, albeit with somc rcorganizing.

The notion of reorganization proved too much for the venerable Mrs. Dobler, however, and she produced her letter of resignation. The board stalled until it had drafted the future policy of the Exchange, feeling obliged, after her many years of service, to give her an opportunity to change her mind and accept the new terms.

She did not. They said goodbye and presented her with a check and a silver dish. On July 12, 1949, she wrote a gracious thank-you note that turned pointed by the second paragraph: "I also wish to express my appreciation of the six months check which was given me. In lieu of Social Security the Board had always planned some form of insurance for the eight employees who had been with the Exchange some seventeen to twenty-two years. Since it has not been consummated, I'm grateful for my check and hope that for the others in my position something will now be done for their protection."

Her subtext stung, and less than a month later, the board secretary, Nancy Senturia, wrote her a letter requesting her resignation from the board. "We realize that when we insisted that you remain on the board that it probably made it very embarrassing for you," Senturia began. "Knowing that you have expressed a dislike of working with boards and as the present board is

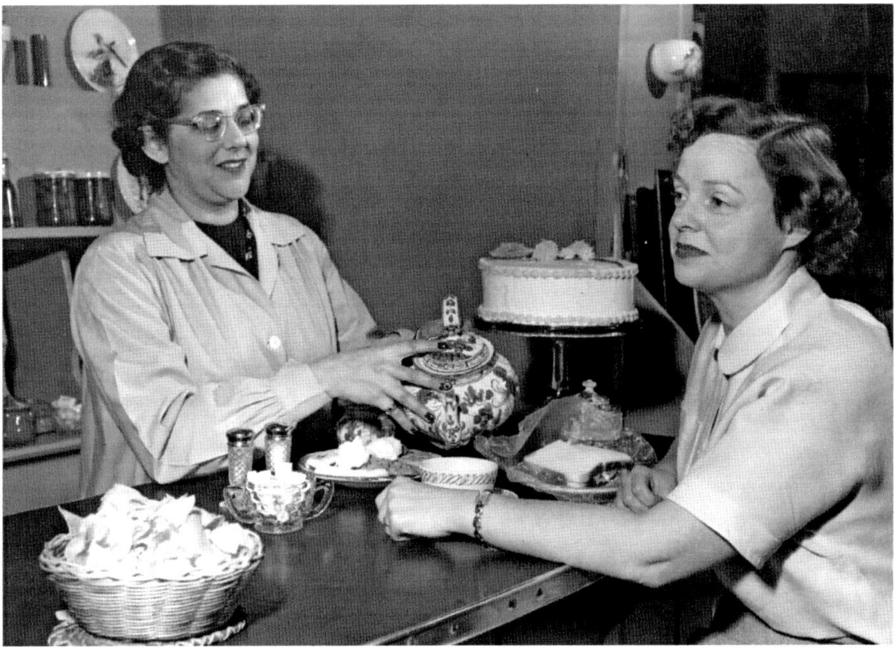

At left, Nancy Senturia, who offered her aunt's recipe for what became the famous Woman's Exchange salad.

larger than it ever has been, we feel that we can't insist that you remain… Hoping that our relations will always remain pleasant."

(In 1965, Mrs. Dobler would give a talk on "The Challenge of Living." She would claim to have increased the number of consignors sixfold and singlehandedly formed the Federation of Exchanges. On the typed copy of the speech preserved in the Exchange's archives, there's a scrawled warning that she "is taking credit for a lot…she did not help start Natl. Found.")

In August 1949, the big sale the Vandervoort's experts had suggested brought $16,404. Nevertheless, the penny-pinching continued. Board members were urged to buy their presents at the Exchange. They also debated picking up the consigned goods themselves to save the consignors the thirty-five-cent delivery charge. On September 19, 1949, someone in the apartment above the Exchange left a water faucet open, and the water leaked into the Exchange's basement for twenty-four hours straight. The board decided to sell the damaged merchandise at a reduced price, afraid that if it tried to reimburse each consignor for her loss, it would set a dangerous precedent.

FROM THE ARCHIVES

A bubbly letter penned in 1946 reads, "Getting back to Mrs. Dobler and her pet project, The Woman's Exchange—believe it or not, 'Boo' popped in there the other day and carted away the best buy since the Louisiana Purchase, even at this late date for Christmas shopping."

By November 1949, there was a slight net profit, with sales in the bakery, ready-to-wear and tearoom making up for losses in the gift and toy departments. The Exchange had survived the war years; oddly, their aftermath had proven the greater challenge. Fine handmade clothing was less sought after now that housewives were buying automatic washing machines and dryers that would tear apart such delicate garments. So much could be had so cheaply that the Exchange's handcrafted gifts were no longer the first resort. They remained the failsafe, however, when you needed just the right present of unquestionably good taste.

The tearoom had a parallel reputation. Sue Chalfant took ballet lessons from Madame Cassan right across the street. Interviewed a few months before she died, she remembered how her mother would take her, her twin sister and perhaps a few friends to lunch at the Exchange "if we'd been particularly good. So it didn't happen very often!"

"I always remember the chicken salad sandwich," Mary Frances Rand told *New York Times* writer Guy Trebay in 2007. She grew up in St. Louis—her family then owned the largest shoe manufacturer in the world—and made her debut in 1949. Even then, she said, the Exchange "was very, very sweet and old-fashioned."

It would have to survive decades of mass consumption before it could be appreciated again for those qualities.

4

Eye of the Needle

1950–1969

With the adrenaline-charged years of World War II abruptly over, women were no longer needed to take over "men's jobs" and help America save the free world. Instead of grinding gears at aviation plants, they were expected to return to the home and fulfill their femininity. Some welcomed the role; others did not. But doctors weren't yet writing prescriptions for "mother's little helper"—the Valium used to quiet any hint of restlessness or discontent in the early 1960s. Instead, many bright women poured their vast creative energy into domestic rituals, and they flourished in response.

American society held as sacred the innocence of infants, motherhood, home-cooked meals and holiday celebrations. The Woman's Exchange honored all of that. Order and beauty were gently introduced into family life, entertaining was made an art and individuality was honored with special gifts, monograms and custom embroidery. The fuss might have looked frivolous to both prior and later generations, but the attention paid to comforting details acted as a sort of glue, intended to keep families from drifting apart in the unmoored, icy modern world.

The Exchange went into the 1950s energetically cutting corners. "Letting excess help go" saved $690. Buyers started looking for more gifts in the $5 to $25 price range—no more of this piddly stuff that cost more money than it made, and no more gift wrapping for items under twenty-five cents. Soon, the bookkeeper would start charging ten cents for each check cashed.

Still, the losses continued. In March, the staff resolutely marked up every bought-outright item priced lower than the same item at a local department store. Lingerie was the great debate. At that month's meeting, "Mrs. Wade reported on the underwear situation. There is a good deal of cash tied up in this department…Nylon has completely changed the underwear picture." Fine silk underthings were stacking up in slippery, unbought piles, ignored in favor of the cheaper, easier-care panties and slips sold at the department stores. Dismayed, the board decided to sell all underwear—except the monogrammed slips, which no one could bear to part with—at cost. Purists at the Milwaukee Exchange might have shut down its entire lingerie department rather than abandon its tradition of selling only silk, but St. Louis wasn't about to fall on the sword just for knickers.

Katy Lou Wade went off to New York armed with $500 to spend on a medium-priced line of nylon. She also bought moderately priced wedding presents—the Exchange wanted a steady wedding trade, the perfect anchor for its fine china, silver serving pieces and unusual gifts. And she bought several sets of willow pottery, the blue-and-white pattern that originated in China and became the stock-in-trade of every British potter.

Next, the senior members organized a drive for young, enthusiastic associate board members. They also came up with a brilliant idea: why not exhibit their clothing and gifts at some of the northern resorts St. Louisans frequented every summer? The tradition had begun back in the Gilded Age, when St. Louis's "Big Cinch" business leaders sat lakeside planning the World's Fair while their wives and children splashed and picnicked. Still (and to this day), certain lakeside communities in Michigan and Wisconsin became outposts of St. Louis every July and August. Why not show off St. Louis merchandise there?

Other members discouraged the idea, pointing out that the resorts were already heavily covered by other organizations. What about Springfield, Illinois, or some of the small towns close to St. Louis, where the clothing and gifts the Exchange carried would be impossible to buy locally? No decision was reached. The board went looking for a merchandising expert to teach its members and sales staff new techniques. For the tearoom, new menus were printed in dark green ink on a pale blue, heavy paper, and space was left to sell ads, adding about $200 a month to its revenue.

The bought-outright committee freshened the gift shop stock with new tablemats, Staffordshire porcelain dogs and modern pottery—especially the coveted California pottery. This art pottery, including ceramic figurines, dishes and tiles, had been popular since the 1930s. (Now vintage, it's seriously

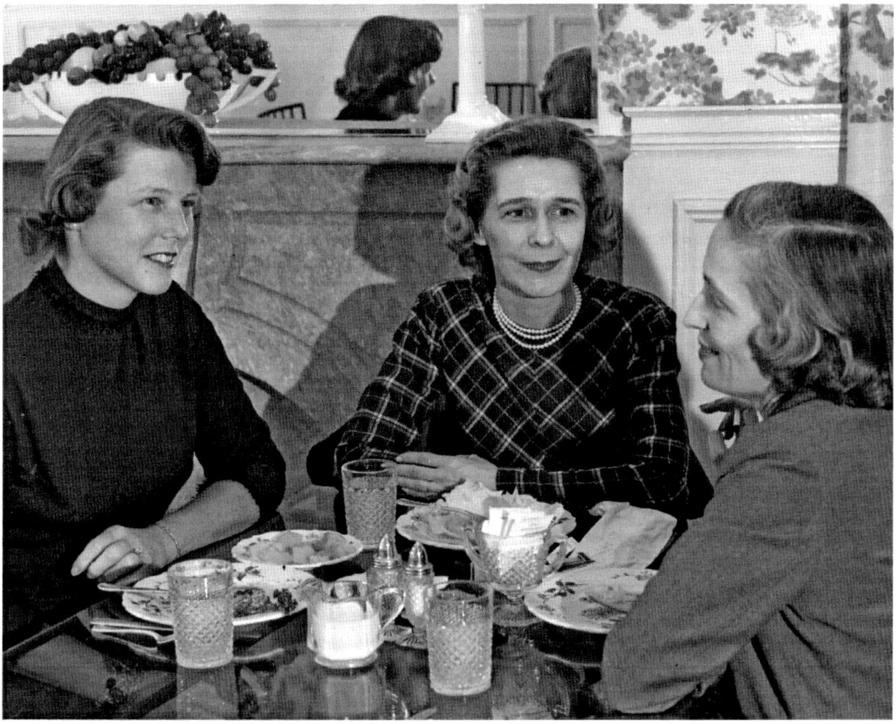

Left to right: Nancy Metcalfe, Peggy Wightman and Ruth Durham.

collected.) The Exchange also began selling belts and purses made by veterans at Saint Louis University's Firmin Desloge Hospital. The Korean War had begun.

Tiny crises arose. Two dresses made by the same consignor disappeared without a trace. Mrs. Ewing resigned after twenty-seven years (and treated each board member to a dish of ice cream at lunch as a parting present). In 1951, the minutes announced, with doomed finality, "Fanny has refused to use an electric stove."

They got through it somehow. In February, though, more disturbing news came. Inexplicably, the inventory had shrunk by $3,000. The Exchange hired Pinkerton detectives to investigate, and the famous agency sent several men at $24 a day. If the Exchange could prove theft, it could collect on insurance; normal shrinkage was only $500. Alas, not even the Pinkertons—whose founder foiled a plot to assassinate president-elect Abraham Lincoln—could solve the shrinkage at the Woman's Exchange.

Board officers also worried that the Korean War would drive up the prices of merchandise and make it harder to procure. Meanwhile, the kitchen staff was "eating tremendously." In defense of the larders, it was arranged that the cook make the staff a hot meal for twenty cents apiece.

Despite the nibbling, the vanishing stock and the tightening supply chain, the Exchange made a first-quarter net profit of $4,800 in 1951. By November, it would average $1,000 in sales per day. By the following January, it would be back in the black.

The summer of 1951 was a busy one. Members decided to paint the backs of the open cabinets in the front gift shop a medium-deep green, which would both match the tearoom chairs and create a more dramatic backdrop for the merchandise. They also decided to buy old school desks, which were popular at the time, and have them refinished. In fall, they sent a business letter to a long list of gentlemen, offering to help them with their Christmas shopping. No more subtle, "bring your husband to our holiday party" hints.

In January 1952, bathing suits joined negligees in replacing the silk-drawers trade.

The board also made some headway on a niggling problem—consignors who had skill but not taste. As the world of fashion loosened and consumer goods became more varied, traditional rules and norms were fading. Taste was growing perhaps a little too individual, ranging far afield in erratic new forms—the colors brazen, the materials cheap, the details excessive or inappropriate. Consensus had vanished. The board tackled this problem by giving new consignors patterns—and firm suggestions about what fabrics and colors would sell. Often, longtime consignors designed the patterns themselves rather than buy those standard, mass-produced envelopes stuffed with predictable tissue-paper pieces.

The "underwear situation" was still in transition, and now other items were lingering on the shelves. Wamsutta sheets were offered to board members at cost plus 20 percent, and a considerable quantity of "American needlework" had to be put on sale. "Mrs. Haertter's tweeds," on the other hand, were immensely popular. Word went out that the Exchange was looking for a bed jacket consignor and for maternity clothes. In 1952, after "a good deal of discussion of the difficulty of buying good pre-teen dresses," the board realized this would be an ideal niche.

The bought-outright committee also brought in tapestry and beaded handbags, and buyers returned from New York with negligees, doilies and breakfast-tray sets. California pottery was joined by California clothes—moderately priced polyesters in Hawaiian patterns. Today, we cringe;

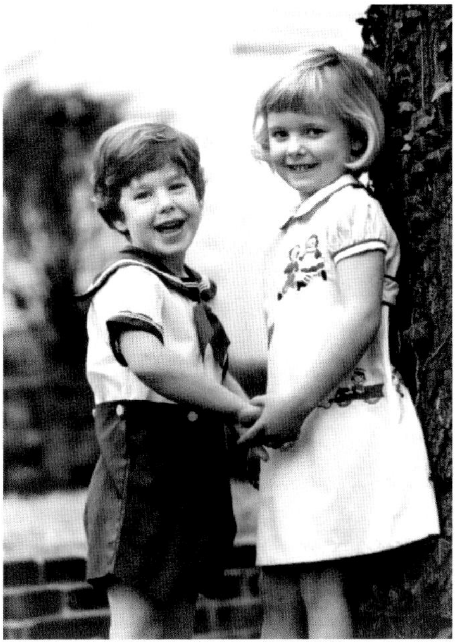

Turner Peters, blithe in his sailor suit, with Katie Whittemore in a nursery rhyme dress.

back then, they represented a sunny ease quite welcome after years of tightly cinched waists and anxiously pressed linen.

The board sighed with envy over the Chicago Woman's Exchange's gift wrap, noting that it did "a very lovely job of packaging their merchandise." But better gift wrap cost money, and in spring of 1952, there were slight net losses. March's loss was only half as much as the previous year's March loss, the optimists pointed out. A long debate began about gift wrap, which should, everyone agreed, be improved. After all, the St. Louis Exchange was a good deal larger than Chicago's in both size and volume of business. More expensive boxes and ribbons were bought (and would be blamed, by 1955, for contributing to a loss in net profits).

Woman's Exchanges now thrived in every major city, and they were both cooperative and competitive. In May 1952, the Cincinnati Exchange begged St. Louis for the name of "the consignor who makes Wexies" (whatever the heck Wexies were). "It was suggested that a letter go to the Cincinnati Exchange that, following the policy they established with the sale of the birds, we will supply them with Wexies through our Exchange but will not give them her name."

Skilled consignors were harder and harder to come by, and a few savvy seamstresses realized they could market their services to more than one Exchange. The St. Louis group now had 322 active consignors sewing and embroidering, as well as 63 food consignors. *Town & Country* wrote about the St. Louis Woman's Exchange in October 1952, and people flooded into the tearoom and gift shop the following month. The year ended with a whopping $10,306.61 profit, and the tearoom's percentage broke a twelve-year record.

No sooner was the profit reported, however, than the executive board noted "considerable unrest among the salespeople on the first floor. Some

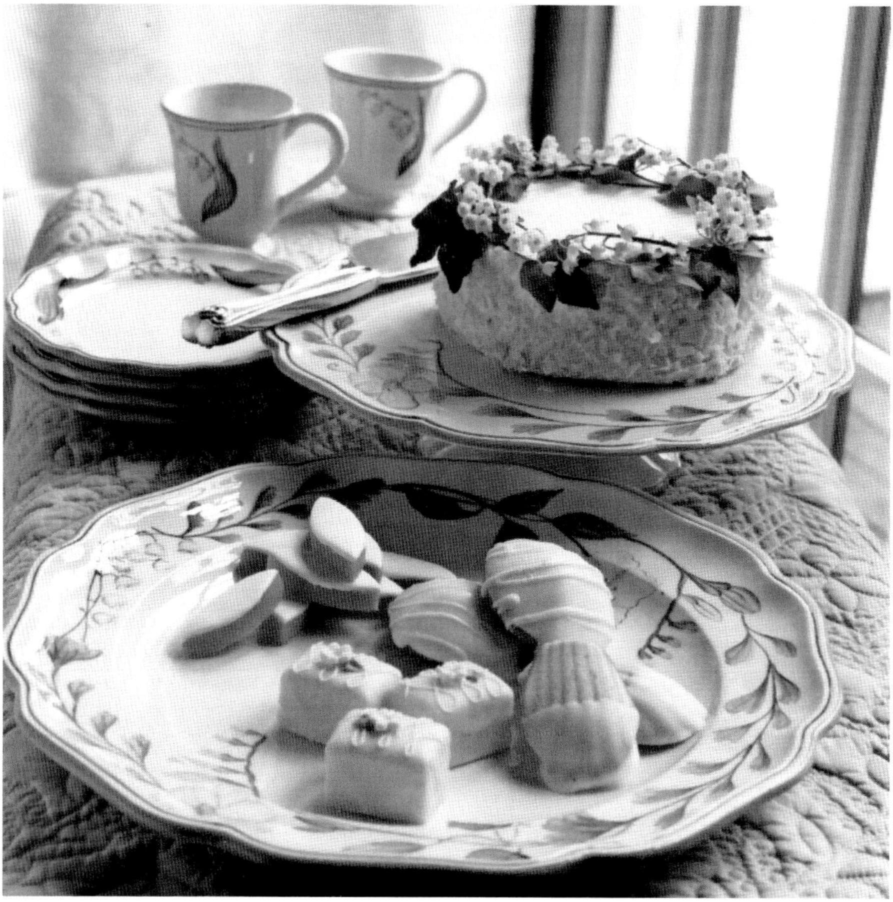

The Exchange paid as much attention to the art of display as it did to the quality of its desserts.

raises are probably due." Mrs. Kendall reminded board members "that everyone must be careful in discussing financial matters of the Exchange. People seem to feel that the Woman's Exchange is making a very large profit each year." In truth, the profit and debt would continue to seesaw, as they had since the organization's inception. There were so many variables, from the state of the surrounding world, war, the economy, the nation's mood, social mores, the skill of the consignors, the quality of goods available, how vivacious and persuasive word-of-mouth was and how busy the members were with the rest of their lives.

The Exchange bubbled with social activity throughout the 1950s. Women showed up in twinsets, pearls and full skirts, looking as feminine as possible. Domesticity had cachet; you could tell by how stylish the aprons were. But women weren't staying in the home. Tickets sold out for "small garden" lectures, fashion shows and luncheons. Word came that Countess Mary Rose Rarnouska wanted to hold classes in conversational French at the Exchange, and a "New York woman" might consider lecturing on decoupage.

In the middle of these light pursuits, a boom fell. On April 20, 1953, "it was reported that several very well-dressed colored people have come to the Exchange." Discussion burst forth. Should they be served in the tearoom, balcony or bar? "It was decided that should a colored person ask to be seated in the tearoom, they would be told that a reservation was necessary," the minutes report. Should they make a reservation, they would be seated on the balcony.

The decision still left members feeling uncertain, and they resolved to ask other St. Louis establishments if they had formulated a policy. *Brown v. Board of Education* had just been resolved, and voluntary segregation of the races would prevail for years to come. In *Tea at the Blue Lantern Inn*, a social history of tearooms across the country, author Jan Whitaker notes that, at the time, "few people of color, regardless of their means, would have dared to enter a tea room unless it was specifically meant to cater to them."

It would take years for the general nervousness about race mixing to subside. Smaller, more familiar problems were easier to face. Waitresses would be rotated so the same ones didn't always get the best tables. Several were instructed to be "neater in their appearance. It was felt that hairnets must be worn by all." Kitchen employees simply could not be stopped from helping themselves to ice cream. At least they ate it, though; in 1955, Mrs. Theodore Desloge noted that the Fauber's ice cream was not selling well, and the cost of the electricity to maintain the icebox was using up all the profit.

One of the last entries in the decade's minutes is a groaning report that the Exchange was still stuck with $10,000 worth of merchandise bought by the redoubtable Mrs. Dobler. After 1955, the minutes vanish—lost, no doubt, in calamity or the upcoming move.

News of the Exchange is scarce until April 17, 1962, when a newspaper reporter described the decorations in the new building. The Exchange had moved again, from Euclid Avenue to 1 Maryland Plaza. The new address was still in the Central West End, but the Exchange was now ideally situated at the northwest corner of a cobblestoned street graced by Saks Fifth Avenue, Montaldo's and the Chase Park Plaza Hotel. Ladies made appointments with "Mr. Buddy" in the Buddy Walton Salon inside the Chase, gossiping under domed dryers. Or they met to shop, wearing gloves and tiny, fetching hats, pumps and soft-shouldered, full-skirted dresses, and then lunched at the Exchange.

They sat on pink cushions, at tables made of wrought iron twined into blossoms. For what was then called "decoration," Ralph Montileone painted espaliered pink flowers on the tearoom's white walls. A pair of French figures adorned the wall above a display case, and Montileone covered the north wall with rhododendron blossoms. The look was French and very fashionable, its floral sweetness relieved by the classical restraint of black and white wallpaper panels. Ceilings were painted a delicate pink and floors tiled in mottled black and white.

Anne Stupp (later McAlpin) remembers that pink-and-black interior vividly. As teenagers, she and her friend Barbara Blair (later Drey) would be "turned loose" to lunch on their own at the Exchange. "We'd take a County Cab there," she says, "or get dropped off. We didn't wear hats and

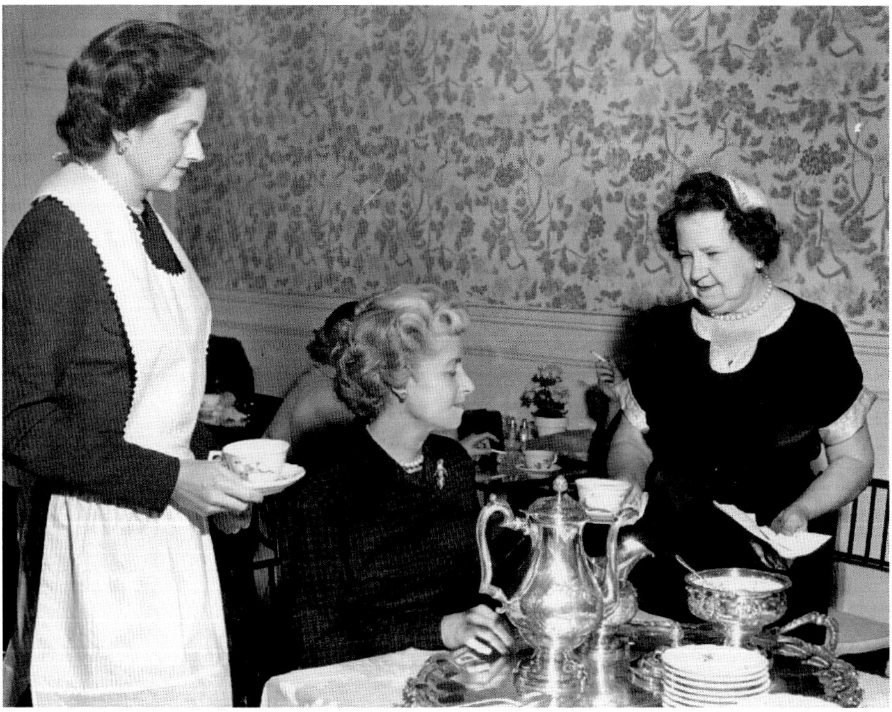

Class distinctions turned upside-down as volunteers donned aprons and served their friends and their friends' daughters.

gloves, but pretty close: skirts and blouses and stockings. There were charge accounts, and we could sign our mother's name. We always finished with a brownie with peppermint ice cream. Then we'd walk up to the Chase and get a cab back, because they had a doorman."

McAlpin would go on to volunteer at the Exchange when she came of age. She remembers it as a feminine enclave, although "a few gentlemen did come in, like Mr. [John] Barlow, because he had a design studio nearby. And I do remember 'slinging hash' for [famed St. Louis restaurateur] Al Baker. He'd always come in around 2:00 p.m. with his wife and grandchildren. Our kitchen closed at 2:15."

Marianne Galt followed the same path, lunching at the Exchange as a little girl and then volunteering as a young woman when a junior board was created. "I'm not sure at the beginning I got into it for the right reasons," she admits. "Probably more because my friends were going there. But what kept me was the consignors, who might not have been able to find work any other way. I believed in the concept, and when I quit for a while to sell real estate, I missed it. As soon as my kids were a little older, I came back."

Irene Holmes says that between 1965, when she was ten, and 1973, when she turned eighteen, she lunched at the Exchange constantly with her grandmother, Tudie Chandler, who had been president in 1955. "She was a widow very early, and didn't use her brains, which she had plenty of," says Holmes. "She and her friends were quite bright women who should have been running companies." Instead, Chandler threw her energy into the Exchange, even buying the tables for the tearoom.

"She'd meet her best friend, Sophie Levis, there for lunch," Holmes recalls. "Sophie had one of those hats with the veil that went over her eyes, and she smoked cigarettes with a long cigarette holder. She and my grandmother used to have lunch and drink martinis, and Sophie's husband would be furious!"

Levis was a past president too, from 1950. Chandler's other good friend at the Exchange, Margaret Gardner, "was very petite, with a sharp mind and a soft southern accent," Holmes recalls. "She was a riot. Really thin, Hollywood-beautiful and smart as a whip, ran her husband's stock-brokerage business without him knowing it. One day a man came into the Exchange—men didn't exactly haunt the place—and she seated him at the board table, which was behind the cash register, and ate with him. Everybody talked about it.

"The place was always packed," Holmes adds. "And women came to lunch dressed. The volunteers spent a lot of time desperately trying to keep women out if they were wearing pantsuits." All around them were bell-bottoms and

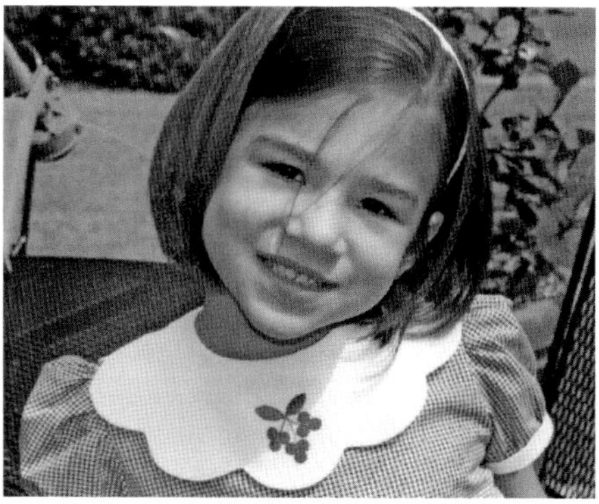

The Exchange's famous cherries could be embroidered as well as fashioned in three dimensions. Pictured is Jane Keefer.

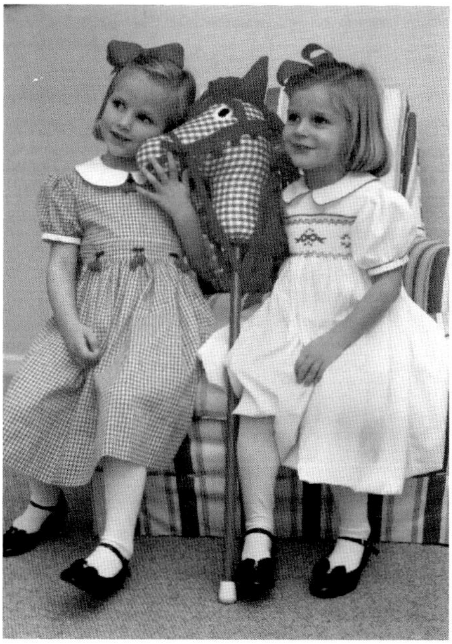

Cherries, smocking, gingham and piping—it all comes together in a way today's machine (and sweatshop mass production) can't begin to approximate.

go-go boots, hot pants and halters, A-line mini-skirts and psychedelic Nehru jackets. It didn't matter.

"Mrs. McReynolds sewed all our clothes, and she had everyone's measurements in her book," Holmes says. "She made all my aunt's clothes, because she was fat, and she made mine until I was fourteen, because I was fat and vastly unattractive. There was a reason the boys didn't dance with me! But I loved the dresses—oh, they were beautiful, velvet with lace collars, or smocked in front with big sashes."

She loved the lunches, too, even though she always had to choose, under her grandmother's stern eye, the slimming chicken sandwich. "When my brother would go to lunch with her, he'd be ravenous, and she'd order him two sandwiches."

Holmes watched the older women with a mixture of awe and fascination. "Claude Fouke, Becky's mother-in-law, I remember being a little girl and having lunch with her. I said, 'My father calls me his cherry to-mah-to,' so she called me that until the day she died." Holmes loved the personalities and the ideals of the Exchange, but winced at the squabbling and high-society overtones. "They were such snobs! It was very, very prestigious to be a member. I married my first husband in '78, and he was a louse, and I didn't get in. But as soon as I married my second husband, who was from a fancy, rich family, I got in!"

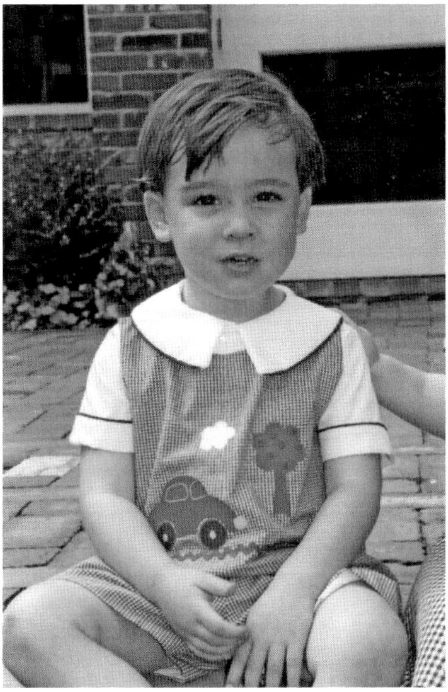

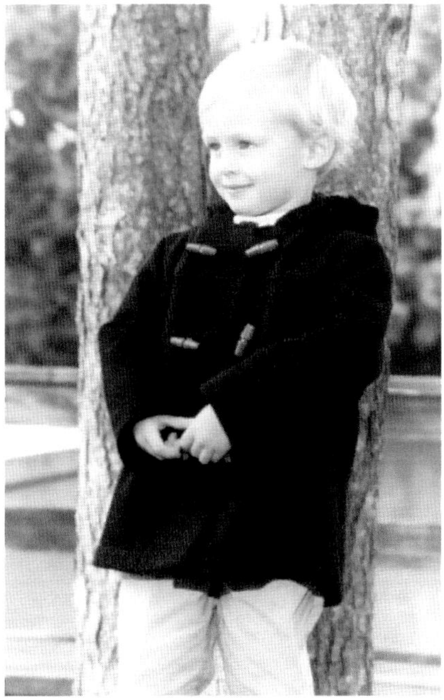

Above, left: Jake Anthon in a gingham romper, appliquéd and piped by an Exchange consignor.

Above, right: Even children's classic coats could be bought at the Exchange.

She volunteered for five years, seating people and busing tables in the tearoom. "It was a fun day," she says. "You looked forward to it, 'cause you saw your friends and gossiped and knew everything that was going on."

She pauses a minute, remembering, then bursts out laughing. "Judy Noel and I would volunteer one day a week, and our kids were all in nursery school together. One day, another child asked Judy's son Jackson, 'How do your mothers all know each other?' and he said, 'Because they are all waitresses.'"

She says at one point, all the ladies simultaneously started dieting—and realized just how many calories were in the famous Exchange salad. "They devised a diet dressing made with tomato juice. It was god-awful."

Over the years, Holmes—who went on to become mayor of Ladue—formed vivid impressions of the other board members. Elaine Eagleton, sister-in-law of Senator Thomas Eagleton, was thin and pretty, with dark hair, tons of jewelry and a caustic wit. Betty Rosen was "divine"—smart, funny and honest. "I remember us talking about bras, and she said she thought one of hers had ended up in the Country Day locker room!"

"Ellie Shoenberg exuded class," Holmes continues. "Beautifully coiffed hair, perfect clothes and she never said the wrong thing. She always said the right thing." When one of the Shoenbergs' neighbors was having problems—the mother drank—Mrs. Shoenberg quietly began feeding the teenage child dinner every night. No fuss, just crisp rules ("Go home and change, and tuck your shirt in") and a steady kindness that lent an hour of order and serenity to a young life in chaos.

"These women were extraordinary," Holmes concludes. "They had so much talent, so much intelligence and resolve. But the world was different then. If you worked, people would think you were poor."

So they poured their talent into the Exchange.

5

Classic Wins

1970–1989

For every step forward, the members brought back another cherished bit of the past in exchange; hence, in January 1986, the return of the "Pimento Sandwich" to counterbalance the "Vegie" (yes, that's how it was spelled). Members also took to bringing in children's dresses their mothers had mothballed in garment bags or layered between tissue in cedar chests, so the patterns could be copied and sewn again. Mother of pearl buttons were to be used on dresses in lieu of the ubiquitous plastic. Barbara Roberts, schooled in the South, had very definite ideas about lace.

It seemed like such a good idea at the time. Charge customers would be called "Friends of the Exchange," and any "friend" who spent ten dollars or more would receive a complimentary cocktail in the tearoom. The decree went forth in June 1971. In mid-July, after consultation with the Exchange's attorney, David Wells, the executive committee hurriedly rescinded the free cocktail. It was likely to create a problem with the Internal Revenue Service.

The Exchange was careful with the IRS. Earlier that summer, the IRS had asked it to poll its consignors for all manner of demographic information—marital status, dependents, income, age. Wells assured them this could not legally be done. But the Exchange did decide to record brief case histories, for its own sake: "More personal contact would be helpful, and we should know more of their needs," the minutes state. A later entry notes that the IRS rules actually proved rather helpful, motivating the Exchange to use more consigned goods to maintain its not-for-profit status. Because it was getting harder and harder to find skilled needlewomen with sophisticated taste, it continued bringing in classic examples for consignors to copy.

The board members also looked harder for consignors, visiting what were still called "Old Folks' Homes" and exploring the possibility of using college students. The Carmelite nuns proved a salvation when they agreed to sew bed jackets, baby clothes and pillows exclusively for the Exchange, and later the board even investigated the possibility of working with nuns in India. Back in 1964, the cutoff had been $9,000 in annual income, but inflation soon made that figure preposterously low. By the late '70s, it would become necessary to redefine "needy."

By then, of course, the Exchange would have moved west. In the early '70s, its perfect location in the Central West End turned into a nightmare. The 1970s were a low period for the entire neighborhood. Homeowners abandoned the historic mansions on the private places, unable to pay even the heating and cooling bills, let alone the rehab costs. Shops and restaurants shuttered or turned seedy. Crime increased.

"A resident consignor of Council House brought in a gorgeous blanket for sale and it was stolen," the October 1971 minutes noted. Luckily, the Exchange was now fully insured. "The price was $135.00 and the consignor will be paid in full and will never be told of the theft." After all those hours of work, the consignor would have wanted to think of her blanket warming someone by the fire or wrapping a shivering child after a bath—not grabbed by a greedy outlaw.

At the same October meeting, it was noted that "Bartender Virginia" was in the hospital and had been "temporarily replaced by a man." When the murmurs of concern died down, Mrs. Ford suggested a new sign at the tearoom entrance: "No Short Shorts; No Bluejeans; No Children in Arms." Her idea caused a prolonged argument but eventually carried. Two years later, Ellie Shoenberg would attempt to undo the damage, urging "that we remove the words 'no infants' on our tearoom sign."

"She feels that as we depend on the infants for a great part of our business, we should not advertise the fact that they are not welcome in our tearoom," the minutes noted. The board held fast until the following September, however. The clincher came when a tearoom customer wrote to complain "that she was treated rudely for bringing her baby to the tearoom." This swung the vote, and the sign was removed. Customers were to be gently reminded "that tiny babies will have to be held, and this is strictly for the protection of the babies. We will get a high chair."

(Infants would soon present yet another problem. As the women's liberation movement took hold even in conservative St. Louis, a few women dared breastfeeding at tables in the tearoom. On each occasion, a volunteer hurriedly went up and, in conciliatory whispers, suggested that they would be more comfortable using the ladies' room. They did not always agree.)

Meanwhile, the thefts continued; $240 was strong-armed from the till in March 1972. Almost as bad, when the volunteers were spring cleaning the shop, roaches scurried out from the woodwork. And the books showed a $2,900 loss in February.

It was high time to think of moving. Saks Fifth Avenue was leaving; so was Montaldo's. The board members discussed going with them to the new Plaza Frontenac, still just a blueprint for the intersection of Clayton Road and Lindbergh Boulevard. At the March meeting, they took a vote: twenty members said yes, let's go; eleven said no; two abstained. The discussion was tabled.

In late summer, members decided to trim tearoom expenses by eliminating shrimp salad on Friday and shrimp on Saturday. Customers were so irate that the shrimp was back on the menu by mid-September. This was a classic example of the tension that had plagued the Exchange since its inception: thrift was imperative, but so were the niceties. In the fall of 1972, Julia Gordon pointed out that bar checks cost eight cents apiece, and waitresses should kindly retrieve the original check and add the second drink. Agreed—but it was also felt that it would be nice to use stirrers or pieces of celery in the Bloody Marys. Also agreed.

Almost one hundred years had passed since Ariadne Lawnin founded the Exchange. Improbably, Woman's Exchanges grew more in the 1960s and '70s than in any other period since the late 1800s, with eighteen shops opening. Yet in May 1973, the St. Louis Exchange's books showed a loss of $8,869 for the year, a shock after the previous year's $883 profit. The shop needed a new location to recoup its profits. But the idea of moving was anathema, especially to older members who'd had the most memorable lunches and shopping trips of their girlhoods in the Central West End. "Most of our consignors live in the city," they argued, pointing out that picking up materials and bringing finished garments to Ladue would be a difficult trek for many. But younger members—Jane Culver, Ellie Shoenberg, Janet Volkman, Elaine Eagleton and Lamy Condie—had enough energy to welcome the idea of moving, and they managed to convince the others.

J. Arthur "Cubby" Baer, owner of Stix Baer & Fuller, suggested the Westroads shopping center as a destination. It was planning to expand and put in a mall filled with small, elite stores. (Ten years later, Stix would be Dillards and that elite mall would be the Galleria.) Moving to Plaza Frontenac also remained an option. The officers talked at length with Neiman Marcus, now confirmed as the mall's southern anchor. But if the Exchange moved to a spot adjacent to Neiman's, it would pay rent of $4.50 per square foot and have to do all the partitioning, air conditioning, etc.

The estimated cost was $105,000. And the Exchange didn't have the money. Accountants from Arthur Andersen were already warning about the decrease in sales. "Continuing at our same pace, they feel we will lose money very rapidly," the secretary wrote. "We must make some major changes or we will be out of business in three to five years."

In the fall of 1973, another possibility surfaced: the old Whitworth Drug location in the Clayprice shopping center on Clayton Road. This time, twenty-five members voted in favor, and only seven opposed. The big drawback was that, according to owner Charles Cella, they would not be allowed to have a liquor license. The property, which was just west of Busch's Grove, had been restricted, so it would never be used for a tavern or saloon that might compete with the restaurant. The Busch's Grove bar was legendary. An old stagecoach stop, it had been a saloon in 1855 and a men's bar until 1973, dark, full of heavy wood and redolent of single-malt scotch and fine cigars. Women now drank the occasional mint julep there, feeling a thrill of defiance.

The Exchange must not have seemed too much of a threat, however, because after some quiet finessing, the historic agreement was relaxed "only and specifically" for the St. Louis Woman's Exchange. It would be allowed to serve alcohol between 10:30 a.m. and 5:00 p.m. The March 1974 minutes state simply, "We have our liquor license."

That clinched the deal. To finance the move, the Exchange launched its first capital fund drive, with a goal of $50,000. "The Board feels that this request for financial aid is a unique one," the fundraising letter promised. "We will not be back again, so we will be very grateful for any help you can give us." Charge customers were asked for $25 apiece. A form letter went to companies, explaining that the Exchange was moving "because of the loss of money due to the businesses which have moved from the Maryland Plaza area, and we must raise $50,000 for building and renovating costs, plus the move itself. Please help—we have over 250 consignors depending on us... We're thinking $1,000!" Mrs. William D. Perry wrote a fundraising letter that enclosed "our new light and flexible credit card which tucks easily into your wallet." (One wonders where the previous one went.)

The campaign lasted less than two months. In June 1974, just one year after Saks and Montaldo's headed west, the Exchange packed its boxes.

St. Louis Post-Dispatch editor Robert Duffy wrote about the grand opening of "the bright new shop." Mrs. Frederick W. Gardner was coy with him, describing all the "wonderful outrageous things" that had happened through the years. "We're always in convulsions," she said. "And most of the really funny things—like the false teeth episode, and the specimen—I would never, never tell you."

They kept the new tearoom's interior "just as it had always been: simple, not too flowery or overdone," said Sue Chalfant. "In good taste, which is a pleasure. There was a desk right as you came in, to welcome people. The Exchange made sure of that at every location; we always wanted to keep the same feel, even though we were always redecorating, every time a new regime came in! Anyway, there was always a welcomer. At one time, when we were really swell, I think we even had a doorman. But I don't think that lasted very long."

The Clayton Road tearoom had a lovely, big glass display case for the consignors' homemade pastries, meringue pies and caramel candies. "Jane Culver was particularly good at reaching all the way in to the very front

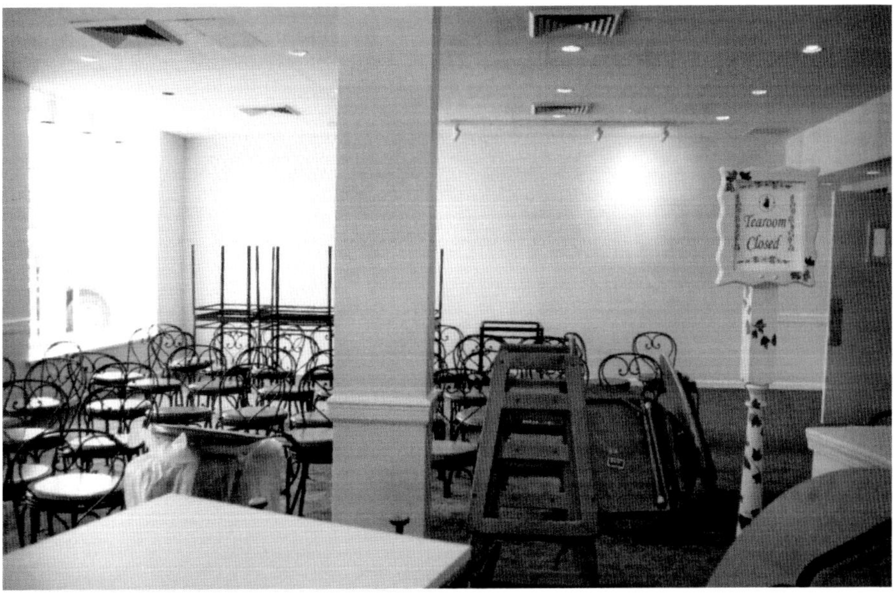

The tearoom at the Clayprice location promised sunlight and space.

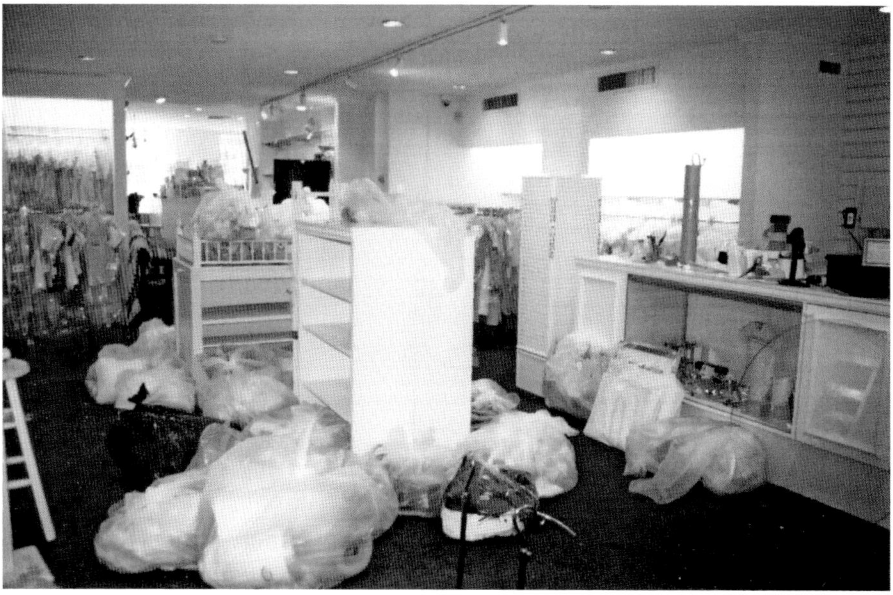

After a week of hard work, this would be the children's shop.

and getting out a sliver of something without crumbling it!" Anne McAlpin remembers fondly.

In sum, the new location was perfect. But the financial problems cut too deep to vanish with a change of place. The month of the move, the board received a letter from its accountants warning that "if the Exchange were required to liquidate its assets, it is possible that it would not be able to realize its investment in inventories and equipment and leasehold improvements." Between 1963 and 1967, consigned merchandise had outsold both bought-outright merchandise and the tearoom. Between 1968 and 1972, the tearoom had outstripped the consigned merchandise.

"Business is good, but cash is shaky," the July 1974 minutes noted. "Bills are being paid with careful thought to priority." Relieved of the angst over moving, members now brainstormed furiously. Could they freeze leftovers and sell them? What about birthday cakes? Could they serve hot chocolate in winter afternoons? "Brown should wear a jacket," they decided, determined to keep up appearances. "Drinks must be tested to be sure bartender is doing a good job."

Still, money drained away. In October, the treasurer's report was passed out "so the entire membership could see how desperate a position we are in." Only one special dish a day would be served, plus the traditional Salad Bowl, soup, chicken salad and Special Sandwich. Peanut butter and jelly for children. Cash only for the tearoom, bar and bakery. "Eliminate Stat-tab if possible," the minutes instruct. "We do have a contract with them, but we can no longer pay for it."

Today, we're familiar with downsizing; then, it must have come as a shock: "Waitresses to be given notice immediately that we can no longer afford them. Also, Mrs. Gaines and Blanche. Miss Wilma will go on one day a week." The ladies prepared to negotiate: "Betty Rosen and Ginny Crawford will see what can be done about the fact that our rent increase becomes effective Jan. 1, 1974. Perhaps Charles Cella, our landlord, will understand our situation and not hold us to the contract!"

November brought the bleak notice: "There can be no bonus's [*sic*] for this year as there is no money." Now they were finding shortages in the till, with no clue why. And they needed new glasses for Bloody Marys because they kept running short. In the midst of all the expenses and shortfalls, though, ideas still popped. Someone suggested they try selling Happy Sacks of toys for five dollars, perfect for travel, sickbed or Christmas morning. A new consignor appeared who could do lamp shades.

In January 1975, Cella ended the suspense and agreed to accept $1,250 a month as their rent, for the time being. By spring, the financial report was showing a slight gain. The shopping trip to the Dallas Market Center was a great success. Mary Cornwell and Pitti Brandin came back saying they'd been afraid they'd never finish, with three huge buildings to wade through. "We did though by working from 9–6 and always passing up the goodies and cocktails and wine that were offered in many display rooms," they reported virtuously. They had a witness: "As we trudged around we ran into Mrs. Schirmer" (who owned a popular, perhaps rival gift shop in Plaza Frontenac). But the real proof of their hard work lay in its results: they'd made arrangements to buy from thirty-three suppliers and added eleven new lines to the shop.

In April 1975, Edith Spink, who'd joined the Exchange when it moved to Ladue, became the town's mayor. She wound up being the one responsible for inspecting the building, "and they didn't have anything up to code," she remembered later, laughing. "Our head of public works said, 'You are going to have somebody go through the ceiling!'"

The mid-'70s also loosened the membership structure a bit: "There was a core of middle-aged women who had daughters in their twenties, or nieces or daughters-in-law, and they thought it would be fun to start a junior board," recalls one of its early members, Cynthia Peters. They'd be grooming future leaders and stalwart volunteers, and they'd be getting to know one another's children, drawing on their energy and fresh ideas.

Peters had grown up watching her mother, Ellie Shoenberg, throw her heart into the Exchange. "When she was a board member, it was just fifteen or twenty women, and it had more of a sorority atmosphere. My mom was very friendly, very ladylike, very talented." Peters remembers her mother giggling with her friend Jo Wood in the basement, doing delicate gold edging under glass, hot gluing exquisite silk flowers, decoupaging wooden shadow boxes, toile painting recipe boxes and assembling sewing baskets to sell in the shop. For all the laughter, "they were serious," Peters says. "They never let me help! They made very artistic Christmas decorations—it all looked very professional. They bought the materials themselves, and all the proceeds went to the Exchange."

Peters also has vague childhood memories, almost dream sequences, of children's fashion shows—maybe to benefit St. Louis Children's Hospital, but she's not sure. All she knows is, "the little kids would be dressed up in Woman's Exchange clothing," and everybody oohed and clapped.

By the mid-'70s, Peters was in her twenties, old enough to join the new junior board. "In those days, you weren't all that friendly with your parents' contemporaries, and it was a wonderful opportunity to get to know them," she remembers. "The age difference sort of melted away. We became co-conspirators."

Sue Chalfant remembered that junior board as a godsend. When she first volunteered at the Exchange, between 1954 and 1960, "the girls were very enthusiastic," she said. "But by the time I left"—caught up in the work of raising her own children and volunteering for their schools—"that wasn't always the case. They were doing it because their mothers and grandmothers had forced them into it." When Chalfant returned to the Exchange in the '70s, the enthusiasm was back, "and oh, it was much more organized! Delightfully so, not overly so. Edie Spink was brilliant—she was a lawyer, although she never practiced—and she was well respected because she was fair. A little tedious sometimes, but fair and quite broad-minded. She'd always listen. It was she who got us doing things in a parliamentary way, which wasn't as much fun, but it was certainly needed. Before, someone would stand up and wave her hand in the middle of another discussion: 'Oh, I forgot, my committee report!' And yet, we were pretty formal, because our mothers and grandmothers were on the board also, and the older women didn't want to see anything change. It was a big problem. By the time I was an officer, we were hearing, 'Well, we've always done it this way,' even about stupid little things like changing a voting date. 'But Mary Jo is going to be out of town!' You had to remember: their whole life was their volunteer jobs, and the only acceptable places to volunteer were schools, hospitals, museums and the Exchange. We'd begun to do other things—I also volunteered for KETC Channel 9, which wouldn't have been considered acceptable ten years before. We'd all gotten a little more aware of the world, a little more realistic.

"I made a lot of good friends at the Exchange," she added, her voice warm with memories. "It's a wonderful place for out-of-towners, too. We had a committee that searched out new people coming to town, had lunch with them and tried to feel them out to see if they'd be interested." The other criteria, of course, was whether they'd fit in smoothly and not turn out to be sharp-edged, hostile or unduly provocative. "When people were asked to be on the board, they normally accepted," she noted, "so a soul-searching went on beforehand, to figure out if she'd get along." But once the decision was made, the outcome took care of itself: "From almost day one, either they were good volunteers or they quit!"

Chalfant was on the committee that met with the consignors up on the second floor, diplomatically sizing up their work and offering guidance. "A lot of time was spent making sure they had the knack to produce the quality necessary," she said. "A lot of the women had the skill but just didn't know how to go about it. They would show us potholders, that kind of stuff. I think it's from not being around nice things. We'd help them select fabric and patterns, and soon they were making sweaters and elegant dresses with hand-done finishing touches. We chose colors that weren't shocking—wonderful pastels, not orange and black—and we kept the designs sophisticated, not overly fussy. It made the difference between success and non-success. These were nice, nice clothes that you could wear anywhere."

The *St. Louis Globe-Democrat* did an article about the Exchange in April 1975, writing, "The clothes have become so well known, in fact, that once two women vacationing at Disney World in Florida stopped short as they passed each other. Each was holding the hand of her daughter. 'Woman's Exchange,' they said simultaneously."

Around this time, Mabs Sanquinette, the original designer of the Exchange's famous cherry dress, retired. Hilda Hummert took over, pressing her grandchildren into service to cut out circles of red fabric for the cherries that would dangle down the front of the crisp little white dress. She made her own patterns because the dress had no trademark or copyright.

In June 1975, for the first anniversary at the Clayton Road address, "Muffy [Matthews] proposed that all tearoom patrons would be given a free glass of wine with their meal." The mood was jubilant, and the financial recovery continued—November 1975 was the best month ever, with sales of $27,286.62.

The bookkeeper, however, wound up in St. Joseph's Hospital with a nervous breakdown. (Other personnel problems were less alarming. "Mrs. Bland said there must be no phone calls for Erick. There is a boy-girl problem.")

Members focused on finding needy, skilled consignors. In 1976, they consulted with the International Institute to see if they might know of Vietnamese and other refugees interested in doing handwork. Fine materials, too, were growing scarcer, as fewer women had the time to do needlework. Soft wools for the baby sweaters proved hard to find, and no one liked the idea of the harder wools scratching against an infant's soft, chubby arms.

The second half of 1976 brought the Exchange a net gain of more than $18,500, although a loss of $5,000 in goods remained unaccounted for. Apparently, moving to the suburbs had not ended the shoplifting.

Another loss of $5,000 was reported in the spring of 1978, this time in the tearoom, an accumulation over the previous nine months. May was catastrophic: Both the freezer and refrigerator broke, the sewer backed up, the kitchen flooded and part of the tearoom carpet was ruined. Then Steve the dishwasher quit, and the IRS said the Exchange had to redo its bylaws and raise the amount paid to consignors. In July, "houseman was found and lasted two glorious days, after which he left for a higher paying job."

On the bright side, they did find a knitting shop with lovely Belgian wool for baby sweaters.

The rest of the inventory included hand-painted barrettes, wooden dump trucks (made by the Exchange's only male consignor), clown dolls, monkey dolls, potholders, magnetic mice, owl sweaters and butcher boy suits. By now, the Exchange had softened its resistance to pantsuits and was even selling shorts and pants for little girls.

The greater dilemma was the May Company's determination to buy the Exchange's downtown property for a mall. The previous September, it had offered to pay between $60,000 and $75,000. The Exchange didn't want to sell, at least not for that pittance. "We could take the matter to court," the officers remarked, "with consignors testifying, but prefer to avoid this." The tug-of-war would go on for years.

There were personal crises, too. One woman came in almost every day, ostensibly for lunch but really for comfort. Her husband was ill, and when he died, she called and told her patient, kindly waitress, "I'd feel much better if you'd come to the service because you have listened to me." Jacque Thieme, a consignor who'd joined the sales staff, remembers how, when problems worsened at home and she finally had to get an apartment of her own, board member Sue Chalfant went apartment hunting with her. Chalfant drove around with Thieme all day—and cried with her, too.

Hardships spared no one. Once, a previous Exchange president divorced, something still a bit shocking at that time. "I think she was having breakfast, and her husband said he was leaving," Edie Spink remembered. "It was right after the ball, and her daughter was a maid." Members and consignors rallied around her, giving full support. The 1970s were, for many women, a lonely time, with friends scattered, husbands working long hours and women's roles changing beyond recognition. Bonds with other women were rarer now and more necessary.

Janey Rouse cherished the camaraderie. She'd followed her mother's example, joining the Exchange in 1975, at the age of twenty-five. She would go on to serve as president and remains involved to this day. But some of her happiest memories are from those early years. "You would do your counter duty or whatever, and then you would stay for lunch," she says. "It was a nice, slower-paced way to do things, and it doesn't happen these days."

Becky Fouke agrees—she loved the teamwork more than anything. Her first memory was going to the Euclid address with her mom and sister to buy "cherry dresses, and beautiful handmade dresses with big sashes and puffed sleeves and smocked yokes," and then have lunch in the tearoom, boxes and bags tucked beneath the wrought-iron chairs. Fouke went to college, married and then joined the board in the late 1970s. Other members soon recognized her exquisite taste and sharp instincts as a buyer.

"I somehow ended up on the bought-outright committee," Fouke says, "and we took wonderful trips to New York twice a year, three of us sharing a room. We'd get to the showrooms by 9:00 a.m. and come back absolutely dead tired at 6:00 p.m., after being on our feet all day, but we always went out to dinner!

"We started doing things a little bit differently than our mothers had done," she continues. "They bought, but Miss Wilma, an employee, would market whatever they purchased. We followed the merchandise from beginning to end, got more involved in the selling. One of the big things I learned was how to make a decision in a hurry. You learn that most of your decisions are good ones, and that makes you a lot more decisive. We knew it wasn't worth our time to sell inexpensive things. We started going for lamps,

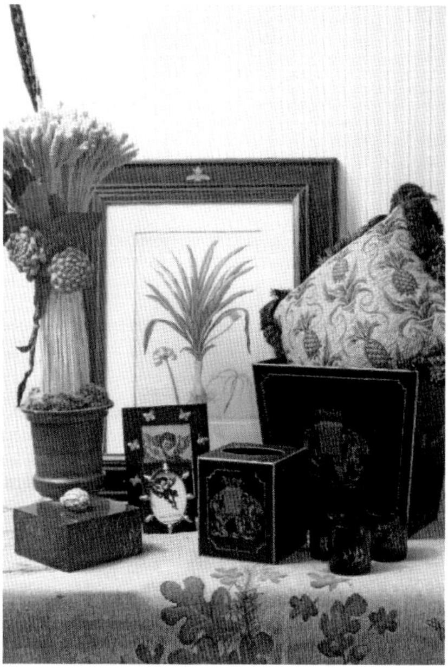

You could always count on finding the right hostess or wedding gift at the Exchange—no faux pas possible.

expensive cutting boards, that kind of stuff, and we did all the displays ourselves. The storeroom was up a flight of stairs, dim and unheated, and until Edie Spink took it upon herself to remodel and heat the upstairs, we did our work in mittens. We'd unpack and mark the prices, and once a week we'd get together and redo all the shelves. For Christmas, we'd spend an entire Sunday afternoon setting up the display. Everyone looked forward to the day the Christmas stuff went out."

In August 1979, the Exchange grew weary of unidentifiable losses and leakages and launched an investigation. "An amazing array of facts came to light," the committee reported. "1. 135 dozen eggs are ordered monthly. This figures to using 7.6 eggs per omelet. 150 lbs. of bacon was ordered in June. At the outside...only 756 slices of bacon (or 42 lbs.) should have been used. Where is the rest of the bacon?" As for the liquor stock, "incredible! We are getting one drink per quart bottle of Canadian Club, two per Dubonnet, three per Scotch."

Armed with knowledge, they grew vigilant. In one month's time, they reduced their losses by 51 percent from the previous year and reduced their bar costs by 63 percent. Sales rose 21 percent. A consignor's ice cream pie was a "great success" at one dollar a slice. The only thing left to fret about were the new boxes (the Woman's Exchange logo was much too small) and the "delightful red and white flyer" that had left off not only the logo but also the name of the Exchange.

The IRS granted the organization its tax-exempt status again, with just a bit of fussing. "This time we were lucky," the secretary wrote. "Trouble looms ahead if several things are not corrected." The IRS was costing them consignors, too: "Eight excellent consignors were found through craft shows. Unfortunately, they don't wish to work for us as we must pay by check, and they don't want any record for the IRS to learn what they are actually making."

At the end of the decade, when the Exchange's new manager received a pay raise, members braced themselves for the bookkeeper's rage. She would not take kindly to a discrepancy, they knew. "When it was mentioned that some of our Board members have had bookkeeping experience," thus might be able to fill her position should she stalk off in a fury, "there was an agonized, 'Oh my God—NO' from our auditor—after which the subject was dropped."

In November 1979, the bookkeeper did, indeed, resign. Nonetheless, the year ended in a blaze of glory, with its net income increased from the previous year's $5,849 to a whopping $44,765, and its net worth about $33,000 higher.

In 1980, the Exchange resolved to raise the consignors' standard share of profits to 70 percent. The number had fluctuated a bit over the years, but when it settled at 70 percent, it was the only nonprofit in the area giving that large a cut.

At that June's meeting, Mary Cornwell confided her dream: a work room, with the Exchange owning all materials and supervising the workmanship of items made. Then its staff could easily teach better sewing methods to some of the consignors. "At the moment we do not have the space or money—but it is something at which to aim," the minutes conclude.

Something the Exchange could do immediately was start dating food items—a lemon cake had been returned in a huff, its edges dusted with mold. This was shocking and intolerable but far more easily resolved than the personnel problems. Certain employees seemed to be pilfering, and a waitress who spent most of every lunch hour on the phone had filed a discrimination complaint after being fired.

The board authorized Spink, who was now president, to "continue to fight this case up to the highest level."

"I had to appear before the Equal Employment Opportunity Commission," she recalls, "and they said we should have gotten rid of her a long time ago!"

Spink led readily, but her favorite thing to do was still waiting on tables or taking reservations, meeting the people. She remembers Bertha Cook, the cook, telling "the chicken man," when he called, "Come out with eighty-four bosoms and make them plump!"

One day Cook, always forthright, tossed off a remark to Mrs. Carnal that she was "not working for her health." The board resolved to review her salary that fall. They also reported that Mr. (Grant) Williams, owner of the

Pappagallo's boutique, was "most exercised over the parking situation. He thinks our volunteers should park across the street. After a short discussion it was decided to remind him that frequently our volunteers are his customers."

The old tension between consigned and bought-outright items resurfaced that summer. There was dissent between "certain Board members who champion either the Consigned or Bought Outright Committee," the minutes noted. Spink met with them and tried to neutralize the rivalry. Ellie Shoenberg, who'd earlier reminded the Exchange that infants were its customer base and should not be banished from the tearoom, now took up the cause of the consignors. No matter how "beautiful, clever or different a Bought Out Right bib is—we must not carry it," she said. "We must not have Consigned and Bought Out Right items competing with each other." She also insisted that the Exchange should not carry bought-outright baby clothes, even if they were cheaper than consigned clothes. The essence of the Exchange—"helping women help themselves"—would be lost, she insisted, "if we continue a pattern of undercutting our Consignors by providing cheaper goods of the same variety."

Spink entered the discussion briefly, to emphasize how hard it was to find quality consignors. "We must not become a craft shop," she insisted.

At the November 17 officers' meeting, Chalfant acted as secretary, mischievously writing that "due to the advancing age of the secretary, who forgot the time, date and location of the meeting, the minutes of the October 13 meeting were not read." They talked about rental space available at Calico Corner, an upholstery-fabric shop tucked behind Lindbergh Boulevard, but "after a brief discussion it was decided the location is terrible."

Chalfant's sense of humor was dry: "All employees were pleased with their raises except [the bookkeeper]. She was informed that she was not going to get one." This was followed by a

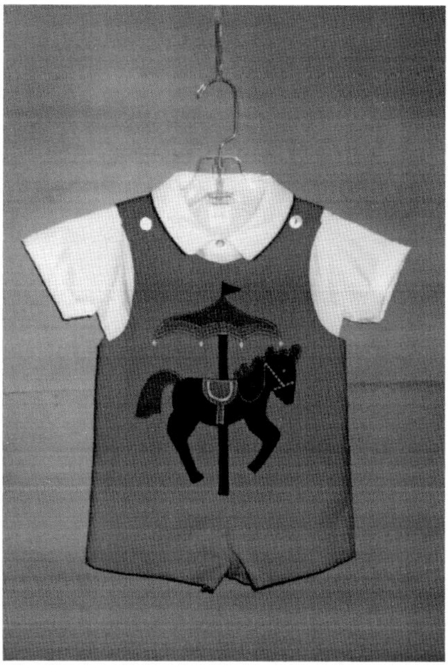

An example of the cheerful, detailed appliqué work for which the consignors were famous.

matter-of-fact yet oddly lyrical notation: "The Xmas windows cost $150 because we had to buy lights for the clouds."

At that month's board meeting, the minutes listed a membership roster that, as usual, included the best-known names in St. Louis—Whittemore, Barksdale, Eagleton, Danforth, Shepley. Those names were listed casually; the real point of concern that month was that the Reuben sandwich was not moving well. There was also a quick jotting at the end: "NYC closing—maybe get some of their consignors?" It turned out that only the New York City tearoom was closing, as the New York City Exchange moved to 660 Madison Avenue. So much for cherry-picking.

In 1981, Jacque Thieme took over as manager of the St. Louis Woman's Exchange. She'd begun sewing for the Exchange in 1974, never dreaming she would guide the shop into the next millennium. She was just thrilled to have work that let her stay home with her baby daughter after her husband fell ill. In 1979, she joined the shop staff. Two years later, when the manager was let go, she gathered her courage and said, "I think I could do this."

She was already in charge of the consignors at that point, and they numbered over two hundred. "Violette [Heim] was easy," she recalls. "You go to Spechler-Vogel in New York, you buy her fabric at cost. But then you might have another consignor who can't sew at all. I'm not being unkind; I'm just telling you how it worked. That was the hardest part of the job, having to discourage people. I'd say, 'We have a consignor committee that has to see these things, and this will be up to them.' Or I would gently say, 'I'm sorry, we have tried this item before and it didn't sell for us' and suggest places the person might try to sell them.

"If you have someone who can sew fairly well, you can give her a finished item and say, 'Make this,'" Thieme points out, "or if she knits, give her one of the Exchange patterns. One lady's husband drank a lot and lost his job, and she had two children. We bought her a sewing machine and gave her fabric. She could sew beautifully, but the stuff she came up with on her own would never have sold." Nor would she have had the confidence to try. "People can be so sad or desperate, they don't know what they have to give," Thieme says softly. "They don't know what's in them."

When she became manager, she realized that giving bad news to a seamstress with garish taste was nothing compared to talking down the kitchen staff. "You never knew when the dishwasher wasn't going to show up," she sighs. "Our tearoom was crazed, just crazed. There were times I washed them myself. Or there'd be a freeze in Florida, and the produce man wouldn't deliver any lettuce. We needed lettuce. That was our whole

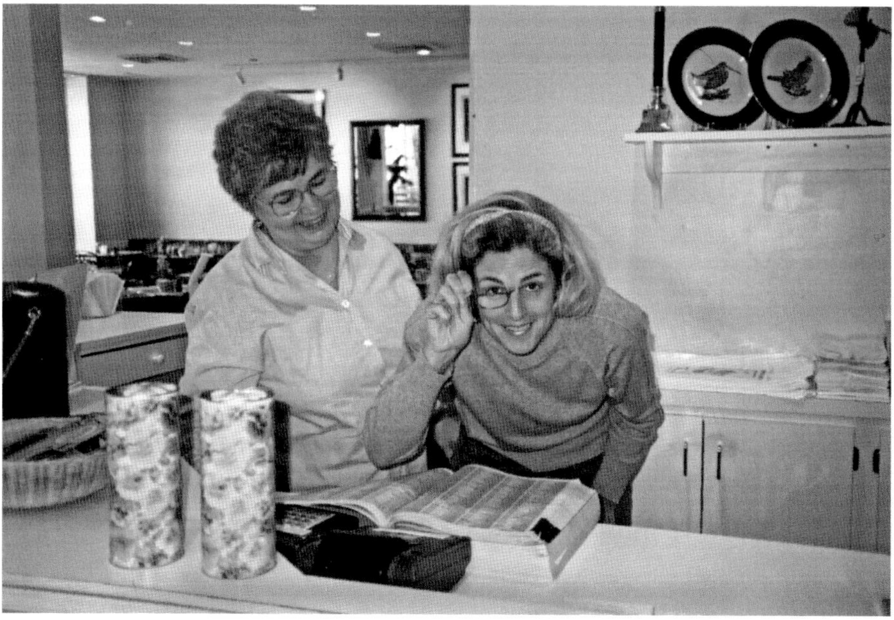

Jacque Thieme (left) with Shellie Baur.

menu practically! I'd have to hustle around and buy heads of lettuce at the grocery store to get us through. I used to pray to Ariadne when we had issues with the kitchen."

She also prayed to Ariadne every time the lease had to be renewed. And she soon had the fun of supervising yet another redecoration. Volunteer Shellie Baur was a professional interior designer, and she hadn't pulled any punches: "Frankly, the shop looks crummy."

Thieme had less fun watching the real estate battle unfold. Now the Land Clearance Authority of the City of St. Louis was offering $65,000 to buy the 617 Locust Street property from the Exchange so it could become St. Louis Centre (a downtown mall that was an almost instant debacle). In September 1982, Realtor William H. Harrison advised Spink, "If your organization and the Authority cannot reach an agreement, then the whole matter will end in a condemnation suit in Circuit Court with your group as a defendant." The building was next to Woolworth's best outlet and near the busiest bus stop in downtown St. Louis, Spink protested. But St. Louis land values had plummeted as retail moved to the suburbs. "Almost surely they will go to the $68,500 I have estimated," Harrison assured Spink, "and they may go to $70,000 without too much protest. I recommend a bit of bargaining."

Spink met with the board members, and they did their own math. With a square-foot value of $60, their asking price should be $133,200.

In October, they voted unanimously to drop their minimum asking price to a more realistic $95,000. In January, the executive committee realized it had best settle for the highest figure possible without going to court. The Exchange wound up making $89,966.40 on the sale—nowhere near its asking price but a good deal more than what the city had offered.

The members returned, with relief, to the affairs of the shop and tearoom. In February, they placed ads for consignors in community papers, and the phone rang nonstop.

"We have hired 7 new consignors," the secretary reported jubilantly, "and there is a need for more." Luckily, the phone kept ringing. By March, they'd hired seventeen.

They'd also selected new tearoom attire: crisp white uniforms and green aprons. New merchandise had arrived—the storeroom was "sky high in boxes." And Juge Gordon had presented them with the oil portrait of her grandmother Ariadne. It was carefully wrapped and locked away in the safe for the following year's centennial celebration.

A safe was a necessity. Thievery had never ceased. One of Thieme's self-appointed tasks was catching shoplifters, and there were days she felt like Miss Marple. "Much to my dismay, the staff was not as vigilant as they should have been," she says. "Maybe the second day I was there, the rest of the staff were over in the tearoom having coffee, and there was a woman in the children's shop. I said, 'Can I help you?' and she said, 'Oh, no, I'm just looking.'" Thieme glanced down at the woman's handbag and saw the sash of one of Violette Heim's storybook dresses hanging out. "Well, what about that?" she asked the woman, pointing toward the sash. The woman took the dress from her bag, threw it down and ran. Thieme yelled to the staffers in the tearoom, who looked out the window and got her license plate as she skidded away. "She was passing the Ladue Police Department just as they called," Thieme says. She grins, then looks stricken. "I had to go ID her."

On another occasion, a thief was caught snagging floral displays from the hallway outside the shop. And on many an evening, the wind was strong enough to trigger the burglar alarm and cause Thieme a few palpitations. "It'd be 3:00 a.m., and I'd make my eighteen-year-old son go with me," she recalls. "There would be no one there, so I'd start up the stairs in case someone was on the roof, and my son would yell, 'Mom, are you crazy? You're not going up there!'"

The Exchange had weathered many a burglary and windstorm, war and economic disaster in its one hundred years, though. It was time to celebrate. The centennial hoopla filled the weekend of April 24 and 25, 1984, with music, a fashion show, an exhibit of sepia and black-and-white photographs from the early decades, Ariadne's oval portrait, a special window display, 1884 fare served in the tearoom and a big party held across the street at Village Lutheran Church. The board ordered anniversary seals and had "100 years of helping others help themselves" printed on cocktail napkins.

The party was a huge success, but life snapped back to normal immediately. In May, Laurie Selkirk reported losses of $8,472 for the month alone and $12,315 for the year to date. Costs were up, salaries and health insurance premiums were taking a toll and there was "vital need for a new broiler." The bills kept the Exchange's competitive edge sharp: "The Berrybridge Shop asked if they could model their children's clothes at the Exchange. They were refused."

BETWEEN THE EARLY '80s and the early '90s, two young members, Barbara Roberts and Penny Rogers, revolutionized the children's clothing department. Roberts had grown up in Alabama, surrounded by antebellum grandeur and refined domestic tradition. She'd learned heirloom hand sewing and smocking, and once she had two little girls, she started making them dresses of batiste and lace, the detailing as delicate as a hummingbird's wing. "I'd spent hours and hours making them," she recalls, "and they wore them to a birthday party." All the grown-ups' jaws dropped. "My husband traveled a lot, and I'd put the girls to bed at 7:00 p.m. and have three hours to sew."

Once she and her husband settled in St. Louis, she discovered the Woman's Exchange salad, the children's clothes, the hostess gifts—all of quality as high as anything you'd find at Neiman Marcus or Saks and priced lower. She joined the board, she and Rogers became friends and they started noticing fixable problems.

"A lot of the consignors were making things of their own design," Roberts explains, "and a lot of them didn't sell, so they were just taking up space. The store was a real mish-mash. Penny and I said, 'We need the store to have a certain look. We need to give them ideas.' There was no resistance; I think people liked it. If they made ten dresses of their own design and those dresses stayed in the store, they didn't make any money. We wanted to ratchet it up a little bit, make it a little more sophisticated and make sure everything in the store had the same quality of workmanship. It could not look like 'loving hands at home.' The design and workmanship had to be professional, comparable to what was in the high-end stores, yet unique. And we did not want New York prices.

"The people in charge of bought-outright would go to New York every year. We said, 'Well, we need to go too, to get fabrics, trims, and laces.' We started walking Madison Avenue, going into the little boutiques. We'd buy some dresses, and then we'd copy them. We bought one dress we probably sold four hundred of. And we'd buy white sweaters and Carol Schrick would appliqué them."

Roberts and Rogers suggested offering a flower-girl dress—an instant hit. They made pretty collars of batiste and lace that could be attached to a very simple, waisted dress with a puffed sleeve. Voila! It looked French. "We wanted to upgrade: We were in competition!" Roberts explains. "We had to have clothes the department stores didn't, couldn't have."

In New York, they were blunt with the textile makers: "Our people are not going to buy purple or these wild and crazy prints." They'd tear through the southern end of Manhattan, going from the fabric market to the gift market, buying tiny leather shoes and jewelry to sell and then taking a taxi back to

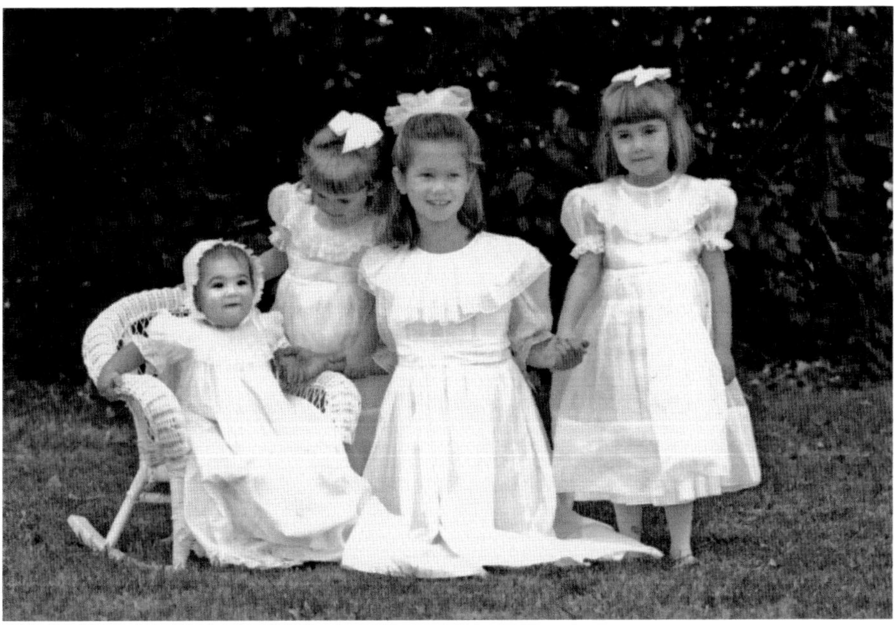

From baptism and Holy Communion to weddings and childbirth, elegance was available to mark the occasion. Marni Thomas is on the far right, Victoria Keefer is in the rocker at left and Merrill Thomas is second from left.

the club where they stayed (it was cheaper than a hotel) to collapse for an hour before going to the theater, their single treat.

The children's department started looking classier, tidier, more thought out and less harum-scarum. It took years, though, for revenue to climb to earlier levels. Meanwhile, the spring of 1985 brought a flurry of confusion. When told the Exchange had to pay sales tax, the officers panicked, thinking it had lost its tax-exempt status altogether. Pitty Brandin, who was president then, drove down to Jefferson City and hammered out a compromise. The Exchange would pay sales tax for its tearoom meals and bought-outright gifts but not for its consigned goods.

"I think the St. Louis gift shops were mad at us because we had gifts and no sales tax," Marianne Galt remarks. "The compromise was onerous to us, but we spun consigned off as a separate entity. Thank God for computers—we couldn't have pulled it off thirty years earlier." The shift enabled them to pay consignors a larger share of the proceeds, sometimes even 100 percent, and let the tearoom and gift shop support that third of the business. The old tension between consigned and bought-outright dissolved like superfine sugar, sweetening attitudes toward the purchased goods. "Bought outright and the tearoom kept our doors open."

While the officers were busy reorganizing books and operations, sales went up, leaving them with enough money to buy a new computer they now needed more than ever. New technology always caused a frisson at the Exchange because purchases were so carefully made and so long overdue. ("We have bought a copy machine for $1,800," the minutes noted in 1981, "and it is magnificent.")

In October 1985, a "Vegie Sandwich" was served for the first time in the tearoom. In November, there was another "breastfeeding incident." Thieme and Wells, the Exchange's attorney, had discussed the proper method of dealing with this indelicacy—which was, quite simply, not to interfere. "We will invite such ladies to use the Ladies room, where there is a chair and where perhaps they might be more comfortable," the secretary wrote, "but should they decline, no further action or reference should be made, and as little attention drawn to them as possible."

The times were definitely changing—about twenty years later than they'd changed on the coasts, of course, but that was St. Louis's usual interval. One tradition, however, was jettisoned with a unanimous vote and instant applause. Pitty Brandin had suggested that in lieu of the usual annual luncheon, the board hold a "coed" dinner at the Bogey Club. No discussion needed. The dinner even made the May 17, 1986 *Globe-Democrat*,

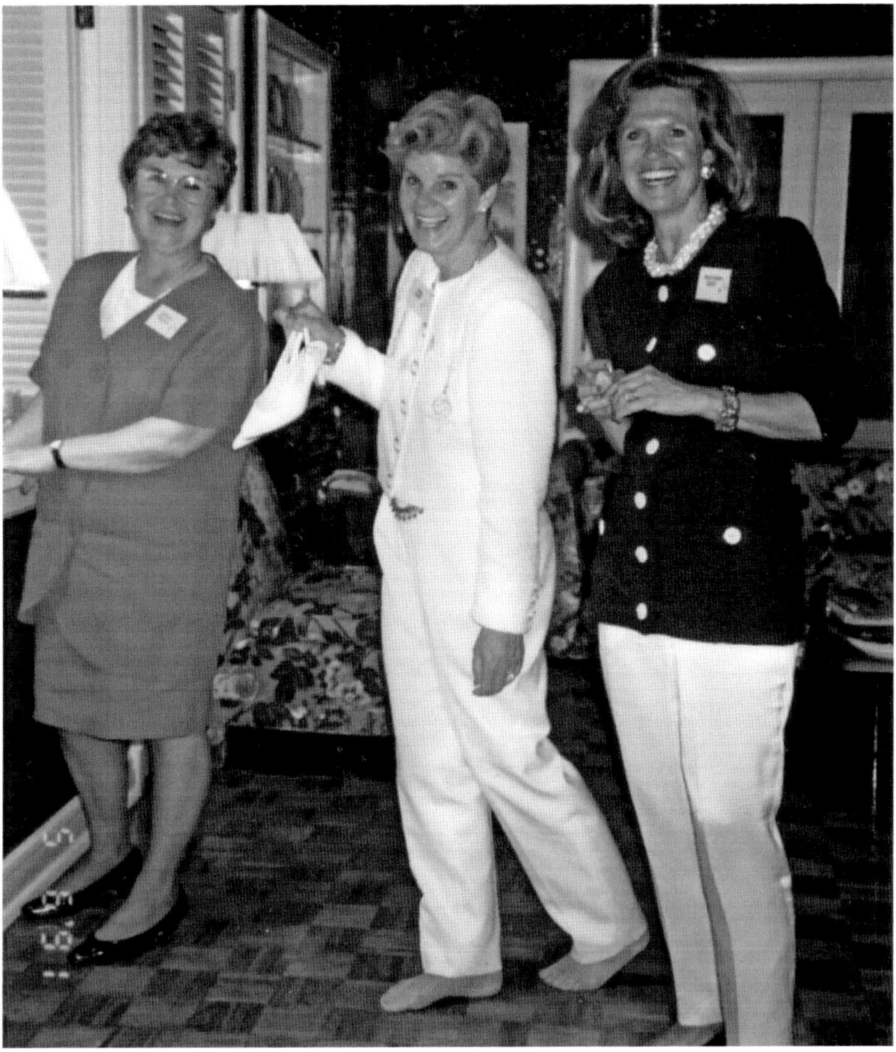

Left to right: Jacque Thieme, Ann Scott and Marianne Galt.

which mentioned the members' volunteer hours (more than seven thousand that year) and said they dined on shrimp mousse, boneless game hen and Brandin's own key lime pie.

Those slices of pie might have caused someone a little remorse, though, because one of the next suggestions was to add some diet items to the menu. Everyone must have looked at each other blankly; after years of the famous chicken salad and chopped-salad-with-the-secret-dressing, they'd grown accustomed to the delicious. Gamely, they decided they'd hold a contest to find tasty diet recipes. Surely there were some. Five months later, the minutes included a brief report: "The diet contest was a failure."

Small crises continued, from "the freezer has died" to complaints that "some customers have been intimidated by rude Tearoom volunteers." One of the waitresses fudged a few of her vacation days and was told quite sternly that this "vacation-day deception" must not continue. There was another flap over parking. Mr. Williams wanted the Exchange members to park in the Village Lutheran Church parking lot. "Mr. Williams' request was coolly noted by the board."

Sales were up in 1987, and volunteers were urged to "make more of an effort to encourage bar sales. Mrs. [Irene] Holmes felt that customers will often take a drink if offered in a positive way." A mailing attracted new customers just in time, as many of the most faithful buyers of children's clothing were now getting dragged to boutiques and vintage shops to buy teenagers' clothes, or simply being asked for their Visas so the kids could shop for themselves.

Wash-and-wear fabrics were growing steadily in both the consigned and bought-outright departments. The women's liberation movement had changed the equation. One of its goals had been to free women from housekeeping and propel them into careers. As a result, they no longer had time to cook in a leisurely way, stitch and mend and launder by hand, attend to thoughtful details, entertain or do fine needlecraft themselves. The domestic arts were dying.

The Exchange designed big cards that read, "Let us keep you in stitches," with contact information for anyone who was interested in sewing, knitting or embroidering. But it was hard to find people with the requisite time, knowledge, skill and patience.

It was also hard to find volunteers with hours to spare. In October 1987, no-shows were such a problem for the tearoom that the Exchange promised what it called "double sticks"—on the tally, one hour counted as two—for Christmas week. Back when women had few options for their free time, hours spent hostessing or waiting tables for their friends had felt like a reprieve. Now, it was becoming a chore. "It's volunteer, so we didn't want to pressure people," Janey Rouse recalls, "which made it awkward. We survive on that volunteer help." Members have always had to serve a minimum number of hours to remain on the board, and the Exchange is dead serious about this: quite a few women, over the years, have been removed for lack of participation.

In 1988, bad news came: Violette Heim could not complete her usual stunning number of storybook dresses because her husband (she had remarried years earlier) had to have both legs amputated. Another consignor, a mother of six, watched her house burn down. She needed work desperately but couldn't afford materials, so the Exchange supplied her with all the fine fabrics and trim at no cost and gave her the profit from what she sewed. The St. Louis Exchange was, its minutes noted, "the only Exchange remaining in the Federation that follows the original guidelines of directly helping individuals in need to help themselves."

Consignors benefited in far more ways than a paycheck. When Marianne Galt heard of a girl whose mother couldn't afford to buy her a prom dress, she promptly went home and brought back a formal she swore she never wore anymore. Anytime someone hit a rough patch, hands reached out to help them—without plucking away dignity in the process. The Exchange was even generous in tiny, workaday ways. St. Patrick's Center, which ran a restaurant to train homeless people in food preparation and serving, was thrilled when Thieme started giving them the tearoom's unused chicken giblets.

A June 1988 article in the *Post-Dispatch* mentioned the tearoom's broiled cheddar toast, lemon squares, gooey Mardi Gras layer cake and that famous salad bowl of lettuce, hard-cooked eggs, bacon, chicken, ham, tomatoes, chives, Swiss cheese and special dressing. "We once had a food magazine ask us for [the recipe], but we'll never tell," Thieme informed the reporter. The standard accompaniment of buttered English muffins was mentioned, too—as were new diet specials Bertha Cook had finally concocted on her own.

The Exchange sold 1,687 salads the following month in carryout orders alone.

At the Exchange, every volunteer was a board member, and it wasn't easy getting onto that board. You had to be invited; two other people had to write a letter of recommendation as well, and then the board had to vote.

Interestingly, the August 1988 minutes contain the first reference to someone outside the usual circles inquiring about becoming a board member. "It was decided to give anyone inquiring a sheet of stationery so she could see if she knew any of the board members on the letterhead and could call them." As the members looked down the letterhead's list of names, Susie Yoder cleared her throat and made a revolutionary suggestion: why not use their own given names and not their husbands' names?

It made a difference. Until then, committee heads were listed as, for example, Mrs. Bruce Selkirk, Mrs. C.C. Johnson Spink, Mrs. Louis Fusz Jr. and Mrs. Lawrence K. Roos. The names instantly conjured the husbands and their work: the head of the legendary Selkirk auction house; the publisher of the *Sporting News*; the owner of Lou Fusz Automotive; and the St. Louis County supervisor. You had to know the wives personally—or read the society pages—to know even their first names, let alone their accomplishments. Now they had, in print, the independent identities they'd forged for themselves years earlier simply by acting on their own initiative. So had Ariadne Lawnin, before society even granted her a vote.

In 1989, the general economic doldrums left Exchange profits flat but improved the buying trip to New York. The previous year, in Dallas, buyers had perfected the art of "precision buying" rather than picking up items as they saw them. Now, they found vendors were far more accommodating than usual. That took care of the bought-outright merchandise, but the need for consignors was still pressing. The Exchange contacted girls' homes, sheltered workshops and English-language schools.

Members had new ideas at every meeting—although not all were as new as they seemed. "I used to hate to say, 'Gals, we tried that before,'" Thieme says with a grin. "They would reinvent the wheel every few years. One time, they decided to serve blueberry muffins with the salad instead of English muffins soaked in butter. That lasted maybe a week."

Marianne Galt groans at the memory. "It was my fault! What was I thinking?! We were worried that the English muffins were coming out of the heaters too dry and might seem stale. I said, 'Let's do blueberry muffins.'" She sighs. "It was as much hoopla as if we'd changed the salad dressing."

The September 1989 minutes noted: "English muffins will return to the Tearoom. Blueberry muffins were obviously a mistake."

Thieme will never forget the day the bookkeeper called the IRS about tax forms, and the person who answered said, "Tell me about this bakery you have. Is everything baked on the premises?" The bookkeeper replied, "Oh, no, people bring it in," and Thieme, who stood listening, winced. "We've just lost our bakery," she told herself.

But the consigned bakery survived, for the time being. Volunteers loved working that display case. "One woman used to line up the cookies neat as a pin," Thieme recalls, "and she got upset if anyone bought one!"

By fall of 1990, the general retail slump looked like it might be catching up with the Exchange. Sales were up, but by only 6 percent, that September. The alarm was a false one, though; a closer look at the revenues showed a gain of more than $7,000 over the previous year, which had shown a net loss. *Town & Country* magazine wrote about the Exchange in its "On the Town" column: "Perennial favorites—with everyone from the Busch family to the daughters of Cardinals' ballplayers—are the enchanting dresses hand-embroidered with characters from children's literature." The reporter also mentioned a special-ordered dress embroidered with an English garden, a tiny name on its mailbox. "My dresses have gone to France and Africa," Violette Heim told the magazine proudly.

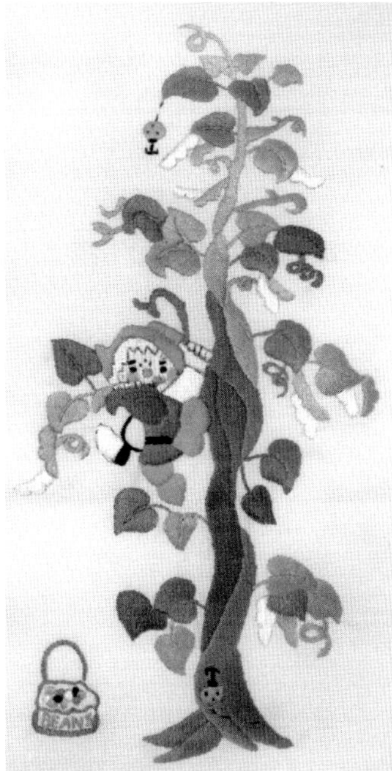

Consignor Violette Heim's "Jack and the Beanstalk" design.

The same article mentioned other Exchanges: Chestnut Hill sold only food, specializing in such traditional favorites as beef-and-kidney pies, chicken Kiev and beef Wellington, while the Elder Craftsmen shop confined itself to handcrafts made by people over fifty-five. Few exchanges were as varied and versatile as St. Louis's, and none seemed to thrive as steadily.

"I used to go to the national federation meetings," Thieme recalls. "I saw the report and realized we were the biggest and the best. We helped many of the other Exchanges; we'd tell them what we were doing. I remember saying to an Exchange back east, 'You live a day's drive from Madison Avenue—you could do what we do all the time! In New York, we met with their president, and she was asking us what we did to be so successful. And at the federation meetings, where you display your wares, people would always come up to our table and say, 'You always have the best.'

"All the Exchanges tried, but there was something about the St. Louis Exchange, from the days of Ariadne," she adds. "There's something about those women. Through world wars, depressions, catastrophes, these ladies kept pushing, kept coming up with ideas. I volunteered at church and my children's schools; that's what I knew volunteering to be. Then I came to the Exchange, and I thought, 'Whoa. This is really volunteering. This is giving your time, your brain, your money, everything. And all, in the end, to help other women help themselves."

6

Cherry Picking

1990–present

In 1993, Nora Ephron set one of Sleepless in Seattle*'s scenes in the Baltimore Woman's Industrial Exchange tearoom. A longtime waitresses, Miss Marguerite had an on-camera role. Ninety years old, she had worked at the 113-year-old Exchange for more than half a century. After filming, Ephron marveled at the place, saying, "It was out of time."*

Did she mean that it was a period piece, preserved from an earlier era? Or that its time had passed? Or, as St. Louis, that it had managed to be timeless?

In early 1990, Marianne Galt, the Exchange's president, began to wonder if the cold gusts of wind that blew straight into the Exchange doorway were inevitable. Why not use the building entrance, and an interior door, and turn the current doorway into a bay window for displays?

Older members were horrified. Galt remembers inviting a handful who wielded influence—she privately thought of them as "The Five"—to her home. Ellie Shoenberg, Jane Culver, Janet Volkman, Elaine Eagleton and Lamie Condie sipped tea, nibbled cookies and heard her out. When she finished, they said, in essence, "We think it's a mistake. But if you girls are for it, we'll support you. We remember when we wanted to move to Clayton—we were the young ones then, and we had to fight so hard."

Galt felt like a secretary of state who'd negotiated a diplomatic alliance.

"Being president certainly changed my confidence and ability to think I could do different things," she says now. "The Exchange was important to me. I wanted to see it survive and grow—and there were moments we weren't sure it would." In the '80s, crafts had fallen off, jobs were plentiful and everything had changed dramatically for women in the workforce.

It was a matter of adapting. Again.

At the May 29, 1990 annual meeting, sales were up $24,335 over the previous year. Rather than coast, the board spent its June meeting trying to fathom PR and marketing. "We need to know how to get the 'best bang for a buck,'" a member insisted. Newspaper reporters were no longer the admiring accomplices they'd been one hundred years earlier; purported objectivity had cooled and distanced their prose. And everybody was competing, across multiple media, for people's scattered attention.

In October 1990, the bought-outright committee announced, "The retail slump is beginning to catch up with us." Declarations of crisis are subjective. The next month's tally showed bought-outright sales up $3,900 over the previous year. But by spring, bought-outright sales were down 18 percent from the previous year. "Historically, we're about where we were," the officers reassured one another. "No need to worry now."

The new president, Ann Scott, had enough business sense to pay close attention, though. She also started the massive project of computerizing all business operations. "Laurie Selkirk and I used to sit in the office for hours entering house charges," she recalls, "and we always wanted to charge interest, but none of us were willing to figure out the math! And the old-school customers paid their bills once a year, so cash flow was a definite problem."

The tearoom raised prices and worked on a new menu. Not for carryouts, though; they had plenty of carryout business already, with regular customers showing up like clockwork to pick up their favorite items. Environmental awareness had taken hold, and the staff decided to buy less Styrofoam for carryout containers. The solution, announced after a month of diligent research, was clear plastic. It was biodegradable!

On the day after Christmas 1990, a momentous visit took place: Violette Heim came to lunch. The consignor who made the magical nursery-rhyme dresses had embroidered day and night for the Exchange for forty-seven years and never visited, at least not at the Clayton address. Board members and staff unrolled their reddest carpet, and when Heim was seated, they gathered round, pressing the tearoom's specialties on her and reminiscing about little girls they'd known who had worn her dresses. Heim said she felt like "Queen for a Day."

A second indispensable consignor, Ellie Dressel, the reigning maker of the cherry dress, was so busy that she had to stop taking orders for

Easter dresses in February 1991. Charming pre-teen dresses were as scarce as hen's teeth outside the Exchange, and its brides were ordering secondary sets of china, like Lynn Chase's playful "Jaguar Jungle." On the down side, new competition loomed. Talbot's Kids was opening at Plaza Frontenac.

In May 1991, the National Federation of Woman's Exchanges held its annual meeting in St. Louis.

In June, the Exchange received $5,000 from the husband of Jess McReynolds's daughter. The gift honored Jess, who'd died of cancer and whose sewing had been as much a mainstay as Heim's and Dressel's. Her daughter had never forgotten the role the Exchange played in her mother's life—or the tuition it provided. "The Jess McReynolds Fund is proof positive that what we are doing not only helps people financially for a period of time but also lives with people for a lifetime," Galt declared. The money's first use: sending four consignors to sewing classes at Eunice Farmer, the city's premier fabric shop.

In August 1991, consigned sales dipped slightly, and board members renewed their push to find new consignors. "We may need to revise our definition of 'needs,'" the secretary noted, "to include 'therapy' and 'preserving American Heritage,' as the Brooklyn Exchange now does."

Bar sales were down, too, and someone proposed selling spiked eggnog or sherry for the holiday season. Sherry won, and quite a few tipples eased the customers' holiday stress. The staff stayed anxious. They'd heard the Tin Soldier gift and stationery shop was moving into the Clayprice Center, just a few doors away from the Exchange building, despite the non-compete clause in the Exchange's lease. Ann Scott firmly negotiated a $10,000 annual reduction of rent, and Galt kept mentioning the retailing theory that competition bred sales.

Which was good, if it was true, because next a children's shop called Poppy's Patch moved in. Now there was a second clause in the lease to wave in protest: a prohibition of other retailers selling children's clothes up to age ten. The owner of Poppy's Patch assured the Exchange board that after her spring shipment, she would stop ordering sizes seven to ten.

The competition energized the board. "Sales are up 40 percent from preceding year," the secretary noted in February, "but we cannot rest on our laurels." Members hunted down Buzz Books, especially for high schoolers, so they could mail target audiences. They also reminded one another about annual giving: "Please save Ann [Case, the recording secretary] from writer's cramp and give before she has to write you." (A

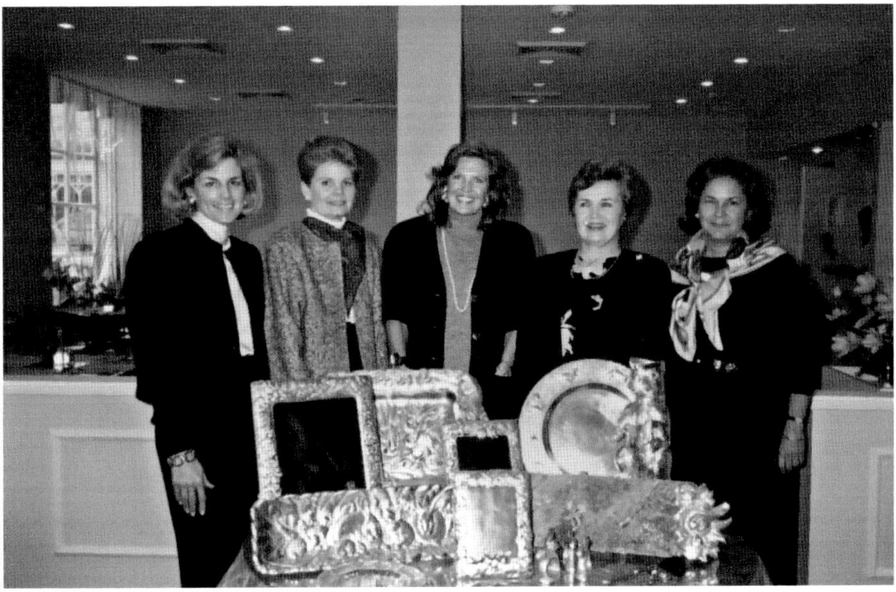

Shellie Baur, Ann Scott, Marianne Galt, Jacque Thieme and Penny Rogers.

crisper, less cajoling edict came in April: "Please DO NOT wear shorts outfits when working in the Tearoom.")

A consignor named Mabel wrote that spring to thank the Exchange. She had to retire for health reasons, but her experience with it had given her self-esteem and confidence. The glow of her letter got the board past a slew of complaints about "the Saturday salad person" and how the pieces of chicken were too big. Thieme suggested they just "jolly her along" because she really was improving. Perfection mattered even more than usual. Scott was about to lunch with Joan Dames, society writer for the *Post*, who (unbelievably) had never heard of the Exchange.

In September 1992, a company called Kitchen Fresh asked about bottling the Exchange's special dressing. This was flattering but complicated, and unless the Exchange could mass produce the dressing in large quantities, profits would be negligible. Board members turned their energy to simpler marketing ploys, capitulating to the trend of decorating earlier for Halloween and Christmas "due to the fact that there is so much competition." Tinsel and toys would appear on October 22, and the Halloween items—even the whimsical new bug costume—would be relegated to a single shelf. Notes would then be sent to former board members, inviting them to come see the newly decorated shop ("and hopefully buy from us again"). Other marketing techniques were discussed, especially "Bring this postcard for a free gift"—what would the gift be? Surely not one of those now ubiquitous refrigerator magnets.

The menu awaited reinvention. Sharon Bean suggested—as had so many women over the years, in periods of self-scrutiny and reform—adding a new low-calorie entrée. Mary Fort suggested a pasta dish. Anne McAlpin suggested asking customers for suggestions, but they all liked the menu just as it was.

Volunteer no-shows, meanwhile, were becoming a serious problem. There would be a stretch when all went smoothly, then a spurt of problems and crises at busy times. "If I'm going to work that hard, I want to get paid," some women said. Others were consumed by ferrying their children, volunteering at their schools, and organizing their full schedules. Or they had careers that required about sixty hours a week and left them exhausted. The new president, Janey Rouse, knew this was a delicate balancing act. You couldn't force a volunteer to work hard, but if she just came in for a few obligatory hours, she'd wind up bored, not excited and engaged.

Rouse also wanted to move the board members toward long-range planning, the very notion of which was foreign. Guided by a consultant, they started by creating, of course, a long-range planning committee. Its members were to formulate a "mission statement" before assessing "critical result areas." As for the volunteer no-shows, board members decided that instead of harping on the negative, they should praise the volunteers who did show up. B.F. Skinner's behavior-modification techniques had entered the lay repertoire.

Volunteers continued to economize—no way were they spending $100, as someone had suggested, to get their grease chemically treated. In February 1993, the bought-outright buyers flew to Atlanta instead of New York, calculating that it was "one-third less expensive." They kept their competitive edge sharp, though: When the owner of Hella's Art Wear in Clayton asked if she could come and model her wearable art in the tearoom, Thieme politely conveyed the impossibility of this proposal. When customers asked for the famous mint brownie recipe, they, too, were refused.

In September, the minutes noted that "the thief who stole Mr. Cella's chairs in the hall near the Exchange and stole two of our miniature clocks has been found and apprehended thanks to Jacque's and Louis Cella's good detective work." The chairs and clocks were recovered from a house nearby. But the exhilaration drained away when the board learned that the house's owner, an avid collector, was dying of AIDS.

On the other end of life's continuum, babies, once barred from the tearoom altogether, now rolled in one after another in gigantic strollers. These wheeled creatures created stumbling blocks in the aisles and jostled elbows as they bent to raise delicate china teacups. Those babies—first the nursing at table and now this!

THIEME RETURNED FROM THE 1993 national federation meeting with a status report: "We are still the biggest and best Woman's Exchange in the Federation in terms of our sales, which are $400,000 over Memphis, which is the next biggest Exchange. We are also the only Exchange that will return 100 percent to its consignors if necessary." She noted that many of the shops only carried consigned items, very few had tearooms and only Memphis and St. Louis had elected board members.

In September, Lucy Schnuck brought up the low volunteer morale and the need to promote a feeling of camaraderie among board members. In October, Sharon Bean noted that many members were not emotionally invested in the Exchange. A suggestion from Jane Pantaleoni brought things full circle: she thought meeting attendance might increase if quarterly board meetings were held in private homes. "Many members thought this was an interesting and creative alternative," the minutes noted.

It was also the way those meetings had been conducted for the Exchange's first half century.

Next, Thieme rooted through old files and found letterhead that listed every board member's name; this, too, seemed brilliant, and the president hurried off to "Kinko" (a quick-copy chain had verbified itself) some new stationery after the fashion of the old.

The great tearoom revolution continued. It was time to test recipes that might add "sparkle" to the menu. Change had to be handled gingerly, of course. Most of those staff members had worked for the Exchange so long that they were as invested in its traditions as its customers were. "It was agreed that any menu changes would first be presented to Jacque who would be responsible for 'selling' the ideas to the kitchen staff."

The new menu, promised in time for Christmas, would include the new, now de rigueur mission statement. A new volunteer training manual would contain a list of etiquette rules because people apparently needed to be taught or reminded of what was once drilled in until it was second nature. Nationwide, the buying committee announced, people were dressing more casually and watching price points. And now a new flower and gift shop was moving into Clayprice! Sales for 1993 were about $8,000 higher than the previous year, but the officers still worried. "Certain items are underpriced," the secretary wrote. Couldn't the $34 cherry dress be sold for $38?

In January 1994, the Exchange received a letter from *Gourmet* magazine, asking if it would share its famous salad dressing recipe. Some members instinctively wanted to divulge the recipe, just for the prestige of having it printed in *Gourmet*. But a young board member, Kary Matthews, brought everyone to their senses. "Are you kidding?" she said. "We turn them down and then use that in our advertising!"

Mary Fort, then president, wrote to *Gourmet* to explain that they simply could not share the recipe—and asked if the magazine would run a story on the tearoom instead. It did.

Next, Fort instituted, over furious protests, the genius idea of a "carryout case," displaying food customers could buy and bring home. "That case was brilliant," Thieme says. "We had always had a carryout business, but here it all was right in the face of our customers, tempting them to bring dinner home. It brought in a lot of revenue." For the tearoom's served meals, Lucy Schnuck, whose family owned the Schnuck's grocery store chain, helped find good sandwich bread. (A year later, the bread would change again, and the minutes would note that high-quality bread from Companion Bakery "was well received by some tearoom customers but not all. Some people still want 'junk' soft bread.")

At the May meeting, Schnuck reported that the Exchange would be hiring professional consultants to help with tearoom, retail and office management. Ariadne might have raised an eyebrow; for her, such transactions were simpler. You just found people who knew what you needed to know and pressed them into service.

In 1995, U.S. representative James Talent introduced a tribute to the St. Louis Woman's Exchange into the Congressional Record. Well briefed, he noted that "approximately 100 families are supported by Woman's Exchange consignors, many of whom receive up to 100 percent of the profit from the sale of their goods," and that the St. Louis Exchange was "the largest chapter in the National Federation of Woman's Exchanges."

It's good that Talent wasn't around that September. "Unfortunately, right before the Food Inspector arrived we had an overflow from the grease trap," the secretary wrote, mortified. "The dishwasher required repair and a stuck Brillo pad was found to be the cause of the problem." New carryout items—spinach pasta and pork tenderloin—just didn't sell well; customers still wanted the time-honored fried chicken, beef and lasagna. But the after-Christmas sale in 1995 was the largest anyone could remember, with customers lined up all the way down the outside hall, waiting for the doors to open. Sales that day reached $11,000.

In June 1996, it was suggested that a member serve on the board for a certain number of years before being allowed to propose new members. Jill Heilman voiced concerns about voting on new members when people didn't know them well enough yet. Diane Reed was worried about "no" votes; she suggested that if a prospective member received a significant number of "no" votes, her name should be shelved for a while, to avoid members rubber-stamping her membership. All this opened a long discussion about what was missing in the membership: "The age group of 30–40. We know they are out there we just have to find them."

Getting volunteers was more of a scramble than ever, with seventy-one possible volunteers and seventy-two slots to fill each month. The advertising budget was slashed, and modeling was "essentially down the tubes since The Ladue Shop is leaving," but ideas for trunk shows and custom Halloween costumes cheered everybody up. (New costumes that year: Esmeralda and bananas.) Tearoom revenue picked up. "It may be because of Suzy Grote's Antiques and Interiors," the minutes noted. "However, there is concern for the Exchange because of her close proximity. She could be competition for us…Jacque reminded us we are now paying bills out of our savings."

Ideas to increase revenue included hosting birthday parties or bridge groups on Sundays and adding a one-dollar plate charge when customers split the giant Woman's Exchange salad. That salad needed protecting. They'd been informed that Westwood Country Club was now serving an Exchange salad. Frieda Rich asked if it was the same as the Woman's Exchange salad, and they told her it was, except that it had a different dressing. "We are checking this out," the minutes noted; whether someone strong-armed the country club into desisting is unknown.

Financial concerns didn't drown propriety, though. When a volunteer asked to wear casual clothes to open boxes because it was such a dusty, sweaty job, permission was categorically denied. Skirts were mandatory, no matter what. A decade of *Flash Dance* leggings and ripped sweatshirts, colored bra straps in plain sight and track suits worn to business meetings had made no impact—except to leave faint horror in its wake.

At the height of the holiday busy season, Thieme started working late into the night to enter inventory on the new computer. The entire staff was stressed—no holiday cheer this year—trying to learn the new system. And in the kitchen—that warm, cozy counterweight to high technology—they'd realized something terrible: "We cannot sell whole pies. They are made in tin pans which must be returned." Customers would have to buy eight slices, assembled into a circle.

The Santa Tea was a great success—especially the demitasse cups filled with apple juice, which the little girls loved. In February, food writer Susan Katzman wrote about the Exchange's chicken salad for *St. Louis Magazine*. The tearoom committee found and tested a French onion soup recipe; now all that was needed were the right crocks. In spring, "Some changes were made with the coke machine which were very unsatisfactory. We had lots and lots and lots of foam." Pads were being sewn for the chairs, and recording secretary Corinne Dacey noted that "Dawn, the girl who is working on them is really sweet. She has had some bad luck. It is nice that the Exchange can help her with work."

Using the tearoom to host Sunday birthday parties wasn't proving exactly lucrative. After one party, total profit was $163; a normal tearoom day would bring in over $1,000. What about opening to the general public on Sundays and serving from a brunch menu? Volunteers would be even harder to find, but they could perhaps bribe them with "double sticks," so the service counted twice in their tally of required hours.

At the May meeting, a summary of tearoom policies was a snapshot of social change. The customer was still always right; that was number one. But

> *2. Yes! We do accommodate wheelchairs—we do allow seeing eye dogs in the restaurant—we do allow a mother to nurse in the restaurant, and—we are checking the restroom down the hall from the Exchange to see if it has handicap access. 3. No!—no smoking in the restaurant—no strollers in the restaurant—we do not seat incomplete parties; everyone must be present.*

Clothes weren't changing, though: "We still need to wear skirts in the tearoom and street shoes—no open toes." And the Exchange would always pay attention to the niceties, like finding a small refrigerator to chill plates. And the staff still needed to be hyper vigilant about security. A woman was coming in for lunch, complaining about what she'd ordered and then walking out without paying. When she repeated her trick once too often, they called the Ladue Police and found out she was a known shoplifter.

In September 1997, the busy season kicked off with a task force report that reflected the era's new obsession with credentials and specialization. "It was recommended by the Task Force Chair and determined by your executives that the first step needed to be taken was to gain professional help in assessing our position and to get (again, professional) guidance." In October, gossip drowned this formality. Charles Cella wanted to put another restaurant in Clayprice! This was far more serious than a rival gift shop. They could do nothing but wait and see what happened.

Meanwhile, in November, "although her dog chewed up a crucial part of her report (presumably despondent at being left behind once again) Lissy [Pollnow] was able to report a net gain of $16,456 year-to-date." That month alone, the Exchange had two days with more than $7,000 in sales. Officers credited board member Chris Kaufman, who had started working part-time in bought-outright and had energy to burn.

Carryout was up, too, and coffee, well, it had become a national obsession, with America finally following Europe's lead. The Exchange wasn't making lattes and cappuccinos, but it was realizing coffee mattered. "The questions of whether to lower the price of our coffee, offer a better grade of coffee, or offer a discount on the price of our coffee to neighboring businesses was discussed" in November. And in December, the point was made that "one HALF cup of coffee is not our policy. Vicki says it is OK, but it is not. She also gives away postage in her eagerness to please."

Frantic with that year's Christmas rush, some of the staff were reduced to stealing caramels to help them cope. They'd have to check Santa's schedule a little more closely the next year. Tea with Santa had a lower turnout than usual, which "could have something to do with Old Warson and Bellerive having their visits with Santa at the same time." The minutes recorded the obvious: "Everyone seems stressed because it is Christmas."

"It should also be pointed out that in order to generate any report, pertinent data has to be entered into the computer," the secretary noted dryly. Soon, they would have to order "a back up package for the computer. The old one broke and we couldn't get it fixed." And while they were on the subject of technology, there were to be only emergency phone calls made during volunteer hours: "No PERSONAL calls. No BEEPERS!"

The board hurried on to a more pleasant question: was there any interest in a Spring Tea with the Easter Bunny? They would send out a questionnaire.

In spring 1998, both management and money turned shaky, fast. The consultants offered an audit, and the comments in the minutes sound almost trance-induced: "We have the tools right now to make a difference. We need to take action. We need a commitment to change. We need to recognize that this is not easy. We need to utilize new leadership. They need to delegate responsibility. Now is the time for action by the next leadership." On June 22, the loss year-to-date was $15,233. The computer consultant was "still getting things worked out…Our professional fees are real high right now… The [volunteer] calendar is only half full." Soon, the secretary would wail, "People are not working their hours, we need a working board!!!!!!" Six exclamation points.

The newest idea for the tearoom—chilled soups—was a lovely one, but it would not save the Exchange. Costs continued to rise. The Village Church, where the board met, was increasing the monthly rent for the meeting room and the charge for coffee. "Bring your own beverage to the meeting!" the president responded.

By the decade's end, all sorts of indulgences had fallen by the wayside. Back in 1991, complaints had begun pouring in about smoking in the tearoom, and a majority of the executive committee had recommended a No Smoking policy posthaste. Two years later, even employees smoking out in the building's lobby were pronounced "most unattractive, not to mention unprofessional." Guests wrinkled their nose at smoke and ordered mainly sparkling water—and a glass of chardonnay only on special occasions. The Exchange's whiskey decanters and maraschino cherry jars stayed full.

Board members regaled one another—a little wistfully—with stories about the old days and their decadent fun. Back when Janey Rouse's mother-in-law, Hope Jones Rouse, was learning to tend bar, she was warned, "Get ready! 'Cause these women—"

"Really?" Hope said, surprised. "Are they going to drink?"

"Oh, honey, you just wait! And not just Pink Squirrels, either. Manhattans!"

Since the 1940s, the Exchange had mixed up a surprisingly high number of cocktails. Men could drink at bars, pubs, restaurants and clubs, but women had precious few opportunities, when they got together with other women, to sip anything stronger than tea. At the Exchange, you could wriggle off your gloves, swirl a swizzle stick against clinking ice cubes and lean close to confide a secret or giggle over your latest escapade. It was a little daring but ever so proper—and the combination was freeing.

One woman, well into her seventies, came in every afternoon and tossed back three cocktails, unfazed. Anne McAlpin remembers "a lady who came in to celebrate her 100th birthday and ordered that thing you had to pound. Was it an Old Fashioned? They had a cheat sheet in the back, with bartending instructions. Anyway, I made her one, and she came back and said, 'Y'know, that tasted like a second one!' So I made her another." She had friends with her, so I figured she'd be all right!"

Now, women could meet at a wine bar or order a Guinness in a pub without raising any eyebrows. Everything was permitted everywhere—and the frisson was gone. Plus, the health craze had convinced both genders to scale back; even business executives had stopped having two- and three-martini lunches. So it wasn't as painful as it might have been when, in 1998, Charles Cella said his daughter was opening a restaurant called Truffles in the old Pappagallo's building, and he wanted to buy back the Exchange's liquor license.

Columnist Bill McClellan rode to the Exchange's defense in the March 1, 1998 *Post-Dispatch*, noting that the Exchange had "volunteered" to give its license to its landlord's daughter and adding, with heavy sarcasm, "How nice!"

Well, the Exchange was known for being nice. Besides, "it was a pretty easy decision to give it up," Thieme says dryly. "He was our landlord!"

In 1999, volunteering was so hard to find time for that six board members paid not to work. A motion passed to stop bothering with Sunday entertaining; it just didn't bring enough revenue. A new liquor license opened up, and the board hurriedly applied, but the license was given to the Kitchen, a new hot spot for singles. The IRS requested a conference about the Exchange's nonprofit status. The minutes noted the board's options: "1) No comment, tell us what you decide. 2) teleconference. 3) send Bob Jackson to Washington DC." Option three it was. "Our goal is to say to them 'make up your mind,'" the board officers informed the attorney. "We want to close the books on this issue."

That spring, a membership drive caused some commotion. Sharon Bean, now president, called a special board meeting to decide whether to suspend the rules and bring in a slate of "girls," as the Exchange desperately needed young members. "We question whether it is wise to change the rules, thus lowering our standards," some members said. "We believe it is not excessive to ask new board members to work a total of 6 hours a month." (One of the women proposed for membership had confided to Margie Tomaso that she "did not want to do a lot of work.")

"Why did the young women have to be accepted as a slate?" a member asked.

"Because some would not join without the others," came the answer.

"If 'Janie' will not join unless 'Susie' gets in, we question the maturity level and motives of these candidates."

By the way, Gayle Garrett asked, what had happened to the woman she had proposed, by the traditional method, for membership—had she gone down with the *Titanic*?

When the storm settled, decisions came clear. Requirements for membership did need to be reviewed, but "like the other on-going problems of the Exchange, need to be addressed concurrently, not issue by issue, as each do NOT exist in a vacuum but are intertwined in the complicated maze that IS the Woman's Exchange." No one was to blame, and the integrity of the proposed members was not being questioned, the now-calm board reiterated; only the process had gone wrong. They would reapproach the young women and would require only three hours of service a month from them.

In June 1999, the dress code had to be repeated for the new members:

> *The preferred dress for volunteers in the Tearoom is a skirt or dress. Tailored and pressed dress slacks or pants suits are acceptable. No tights, leggings, Capri pants, chinos, khakis, jeans, shorts, or skorts are allowed. Dress shoes are required. Sneakers, boat shoes, and sandals are not permitted.*

On June 28, the Exchange celebrated the twenty-fifth anniversary of its beloved cook, Bertha Cook. The kitchen staff she'd mentored so patiently decorated a poster board with sparkle paint, and at the end of the festivities, President Sharon Bean and Jacque Thieme gave her a check. "She seemed blown away," they reported happily. She was probably less so two months later when the baker gave two weeks' notice. Cook had filled in the previous time a baker vanished, baking all the brownies and lemon squares on top of her usual workload. Now, she was also about to lose another member of her staff, who had be out for a hysterectomy and six weeks' recovery.

On September 20, the minutes noted, "Our mission of helping others help themselves will be increasingly in the social mainstream as the government continues to pull back its assistance programs." Lawyer Bob Jackson recommended updating the Articles of Incorporation to make them gender neutral, a slightly ironic change in an organization that had always been run by women, and largely for women, although there was that nice gentleman consignor who made wooden toys. Best to join the century, though.

October 30 was the Exchange's last day to serve liquor, and volunteers did so with a flourish.

In November, new ideas (baby doll cherry dresses and holiday jammies) joined the old (button-on Mary Jane shoes in black patent leather and red leather). The holidays went fairly smoothly, with doughnuts and other treats sweetening the mornings of hectic workdays. A new ease with computers was showing up in casual comments. ("Martha's stuff is all on Windows

THE BOARD ON MAY 19, 1999

Mrs. Donald W. Anthon, Chairman
Mrs. William N. Bean, President
Mrs. Edward T. Baur, Executive Vice-President
Mrs. Timothy G. Hennessey, Treasurer
Mrs. Bettye Y. Kerckhoff, Assistant Treasurer
Mrs. Ralph G. Dacey Jr., Recording Secretary
Mrs. Richard T. Terry, Corresponding Secretary
Mrs. Lawrence A. Reed, Chairman, Public Relations
Mrs. Garth F. Fort, Co-Chairman, Office Operations
Mrs. Fairfax Pollnow, Co-Chairman, Office Operations
Mrs. Lea Luchetti, Chairman, Human Resources
Mrs. Jonathan Panteleoni, Chairman, Funding/Special Events
Mrs. Maury Matthews, Chairman, Shop
Mrs. Karl J. Heilman, Chairman, Advertising
Mrs. Richard G. Millman, Chairman, Bought Outright
Mrs. Holt Tipton, Chairman, Consigned
Mrs. Oscar Horan, Chairman, Tearoom
Mrs. James T. Chamness Jr., Member-at-Large
Mrs. Garth F. Fort, Member-at-Large
Mrs. Martin Galt III, Member-at-Large
Mrs. Ernest T. Rouse III, Member-at-Large
Mrs. Hugh Scott III, Member-at-Large

now—Microsoft Word.") Then, in early December, the Exchange was robbed. The son of one of the cleaning service crew members broke in, and he and his friends managed to steal about $4,000 from the safe. By the time the police tracked them down, they'd already spent some of the money on fancy clothes, drugs and food. What was left was returned to the safe.

The board continued preparations for Tea with Santa.

IN 2000, KARY MATTHEWS became president. She would have to bring the Exchange into the twenty-first century. "We didn't have a business plan, we didn't have any kind of formatting for advertising and we didn't have a budget," she recalls, wincing. "We are three distinct entities: a restaurant, a retail operation and a not-for-profit. Those are different tax structures and different operational procedures.

"It was a lot of work," she admits. "But I loved it. I also had a hand in getting us online, and that was really exhilarating." She had no web, business or technology background herself, so she continued the Exchange's time-honored strategy: find experts in other fields to advise you.

"Like Larry Honig [CEO of the company that owned Macy's and Bloomingdale's]," Matthews says, a hint of laughter already in her voice. "His wife, Ellen, was a member for a brief shining moment. We asked Larry, as a favor, to take a look at our books and tell us how we could improve. He spent days there, even brought in an accountant from the May Company. In the end, he said, 'Ladies, I don't know how the hell you stay in business. This should be a Harvard Business School case study, because you cannot possibly survive doing what you're doing, but somehow you are!'"

Matthews knew exactly how: "Love and attention. A lot of caring, a lot of people bringing their individual talents together and working toward a common goal. When I first came on board, I was a new mother with a screaming, colicky baby. I couldn't wait to do my table wait. I met some women in their late thirties who had just that much more experience with kids and life. We would do our work and then stay for lunch and talk. Some of my best recipes and kid tips came out of those lunches."

She points out that the Exchange "has existed without change of purpose for more than a century. It's been able to provide millions of dollars over the years, very quietly and not as a handout. When the number of women who knew how to appliqué fell off and became almost nonexistent, we bought women sewing machines and taught them. Pretty much every penny went to help the consignors because there was no bureaucracy to feed. Volunteers would buy the stuff, unpack it, mark it, display it, sell it and wrap it."

Matthews was fascinated by the consignors' life stories, and she bent the old code of anonymity just a little, using their first names to tell members a bit about them in the Exchange newsletter. "Some would literally plow the fields during the day, raise their children, help them with their homework and then stay up until the wee hours of the night making pumpkin suits," she says. "These are women who are brave and courageous beyond imagining. They don't whine, and they don't mope. They get down to it."

The purpose of the Exchange was more obvious after the Civil War, when penniless widows were ashamed to work and afraid of the factories. But the need hadn't lessened. Linda's husband was a farmer who died of a heart attack. Mary Ann had two children and an alcoholic husband who could

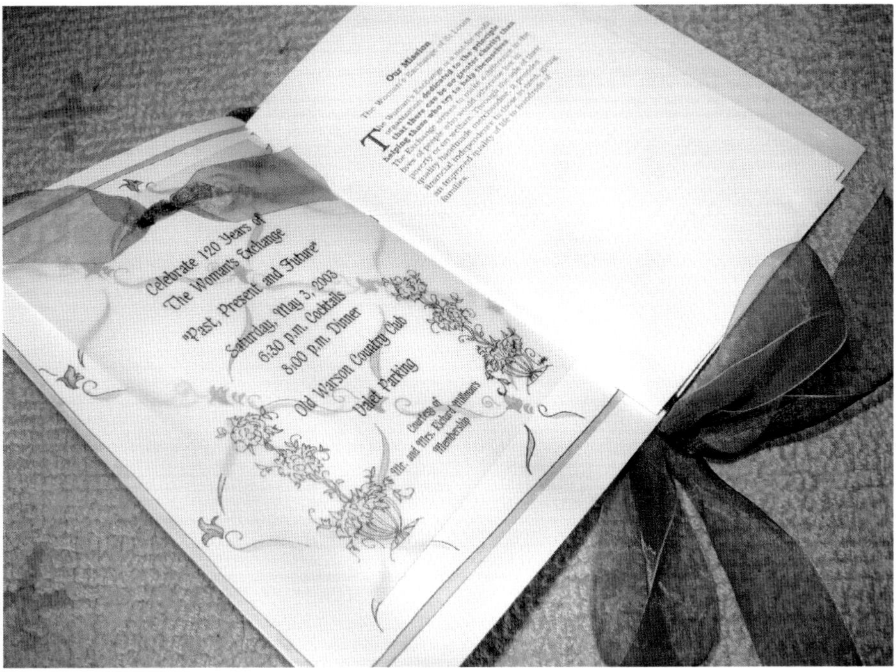

The program for the 120th anniversary.

not hold a job and totaled their car (she eventually divorced him). Carol's son was diagnosed with leukemia; she left her full-time job to take care of him, and then her husband lost his job. There was a ninety-year-old widow who crocheted children's toys, a young woman trying to put herself through college, a mother of five whose husband was a seminary student and a retired couple who were supporting a son with cognitive disabilities.

Every year brought more stories. One mother knitted for travel money. Her sons, both marines, were injured in Iraq. One was paralyzed, and the other suffered a severe head injury, and they live on opposite coasts. Another consigner had several disabilities herself, including congestive heart failure and limited mobility, which prevented her from working outside her home.

The world was still full of women trying to take care of their families or support themselves against huge odds. Today's shame might be domestic violence or alcoholism or not speaking English; the reason for working at home might be a fragile nervous system or a child with an intellectual disability.

Everything had changed and nothing had changed.

IN 2003, THE EXCHANGE turned 120, and its mainstay for decades, manager Jacque Thieme, turned 70. With tears in her eyes, she announced that it was time for her to retire. The volunteers pulled themselves out of their shock by planning the most smashing party they could imagine. They sent a limo to pick up Thieme and her family and drive them to Old Warson Country Club, where dinner would pass even her high standards and a trio was waiting to serenade her.

"People hung around even after the party dispersed," recalls Tara Lewis, a lawyer who was then vice-president of the Exchange. "We fundraised a nice pension for her, raised $23,000 for her twenty-three years of service. We also gave her airline tickets—we wanted to send her to Europe because she loves history.

"That evening was a high spot," Lewis says, an odd note coming into her voice. "We celebrated not only Jacque but the Exchange, because they were inseparable. I think we were lulled into a sense of complacency.

"And then came the crisis."

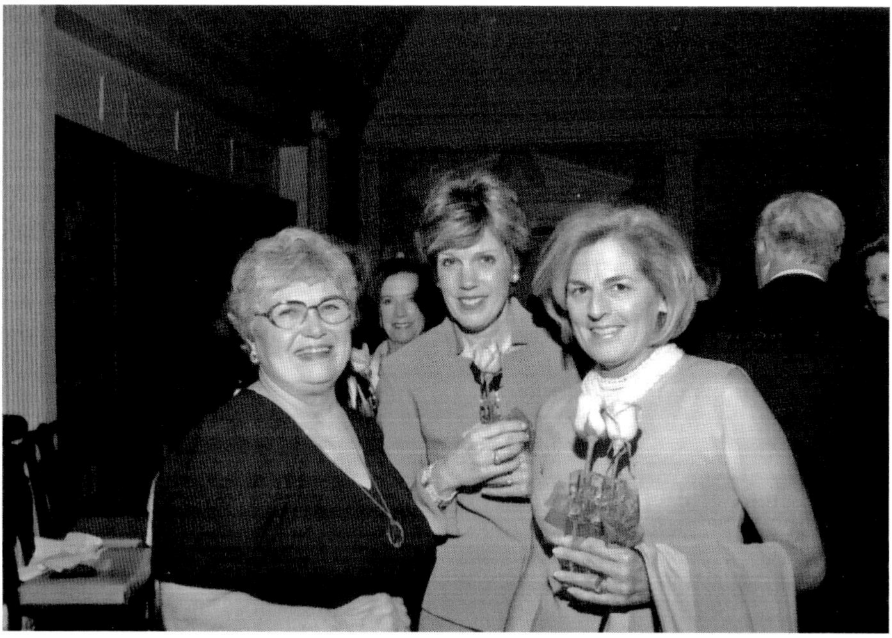

Jacque Thieme, Janey Rouse and Shellie Baur at Thieme's thank-you party.

Lewis first heard about the Exchange in 1996, when a friend said, "I would like to propose you for membership."

"Oh, OK," said Lewis, always cheerful. "What's the Woman's Exchange?" She found out, to her mortification, that she lived right around the corner from this bit of history. "I didn't grow up in St. Louis," she explains. "So my daughter never had a cherry dress!"

She did her table waits and showed up for meetings. "Then, out of the blue, I was asked to be vice-president," she says. That meant, according to the Exchange bylaws, that she would serve two years as vice-president, two years as president and two years chairing the board.

"My experience was unique," she continues wryly, "because we were broke when I took over." After Thieme left, they had hired a new manager who had somehow blown through their entire savings. "She hired an accountant, and I don't know what that woman did, but it was a disaster." Lewis sighs. She'd worked on the strategic plan, and she was looking forward to coming in as president and implementing it. Instead, she got a call from the bookkeeper straightaway, asking her to sign a withdrawal from savings.

"Why?" Lewis asked. She was told there was no other money for payroll, and they had only six to eight weeks of operating funds left. "Put the checkbook away," she directed. "I'm not signing anything until I get more information."

She and the other officers went back through all the checks already written. "We couldn't find any theft or anything," she says, "but the money was gone. We were scared to death." The past presidents advised her to say nothing that might panic the general membership. "So at the end of July, I'm just supposed to send everyone a letter saying that we're gone?" she retorted. She called an emergency meeting and unfolded the details of the crisis. Members authorized her to create a finance committee and a management committee that would work through the summer and then take stock again. Meanwhile, they shortened store hours, let one employee go and stopped spending.

As soon as those finance and management committees were formed, Lewis invited their members to a meeting at her house. Once everyone was seated, she looked around the room and said, "OK, are we going to let it go or are we going to support it? And if we're going to support it, get out your checkbooks." At their next meeting, they received a $100,000 anonymous gift. Then they raised another $90,000.

"It showed me there was a real love for this organization," Lewis says softly. "Some of the others hesitated to put money into a dying organization, but when they saw we were going to make it, they came back.

"We were lean as we could be," she continues. "We didn't have a manager; we didn't have money to hire one. But by fall, we were still in business. We put that $100,000 donation in our savings account, and I locked it up. I said, 'Two board members have to sign before anyone can draw any money out.' The bank gave us a working capital loan of $100,000 based on the strength of that, so at least we had a little bit more working capital. We had pushed the waterfall back just a little bit."

The Exchange went another entire year without a manager. "I was over there forty hours a week at least," Lewis says, "and then I'd come home and close myself into the study and work there. My kids would all be lined up when I came out."

In summer 2005, the board placed a detailed employment ad in the newspaper. The job of managing the Exchange was hardly typical. It needed someone capable of supervising a restaurant, a retail business and a nonprofit—and it couldn't pay much.

"Jessica was so obviously perfect," Lewis recalls happily. Jessica Wright had been supervising a Washington University bookstore with a Starbucks in it. "She wrote a beautifully articulated explanation of why she met our criteria. We got her in immediately for an interview." She smiles. "And she had a couple of piercings in her ear, and she was very young."

Amused, Lewis thought of the contrast to their beloved Jacquc. They'd have to adapt. This young woman was too good to let go.

"Don't tell her about our financial situation," board members urged Lewis.

"Are you crazy?" she replied, the phrase now reflexive.

When she told Wright all the gory details, Wright looked at her, smiled and said, "I love a good challenge."

THE BOARD STAYED MORE involved than it had been in the past, and Lewis let go very slowly. Every time she eased up on the rope, Wright capably took up the slack. She quickly grasped the need to preserve tradition, but she snuck in as many improvements as she could. "Like stratifying our price points," she says. "We really used to be only a high-end shop. Now you can get an inexpensive hostess gift or find a gift for your child's teacher without spending $200. And we're recognizing that people are more casual in the way that they dress their children and the way they entertain. Nobody wants to polish sterling anymore. Personally, I don't want to use china that can't go in the dishwasher. And I don't feel a need for finger bowls."

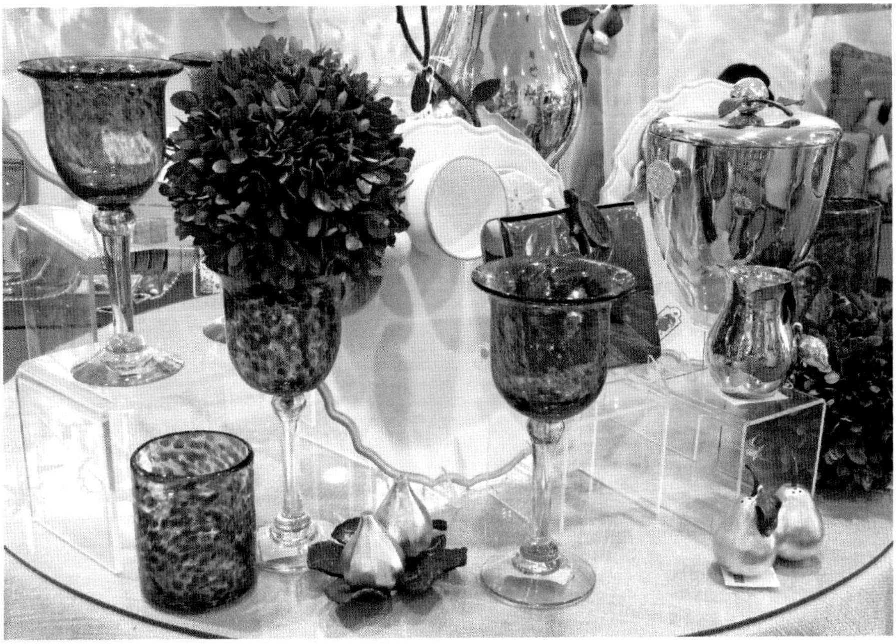

A century ago, you'd see silver that had to be polished; today's low-maintenance tableware and serving pieces are more about art than convention.

The general relaxation didn't mean the Exchange would forsake gorgeous, high-quality gifts. "When we find something done with artistry, something extraordinary and beautiful, we know people will understand the value," Wright says. "But overall, people are spending less money on the way they entertain at home. We're carrying more personal accessories, hats and jewelry, and more play clothes for kids. The cherry dress is wonderful, and it's always going to sell, but people don't put that on their little girl to go play in the yard, and they still want something cute.

"They're also excited to find age-appropriate adorable play clothes," she adds. "In department stores, children's clothes are miniature replicas of adult clothes. We're not trying to be overly prim, but children are children. Of course, we want them to like our clothes, too—that's always the challenge, because children want to wear what other children are wearing. We are very careful to strike that balance. We pay attention to color and fabric and cut; we know an older child isn't going to want a Peter Pan collar, for example, so we don't even bother. We don't want arguments between parent and child. If a dress has no sleeves, you don't have to worry about whether they are puffed or not, and you have something that looks a little more grown-up but

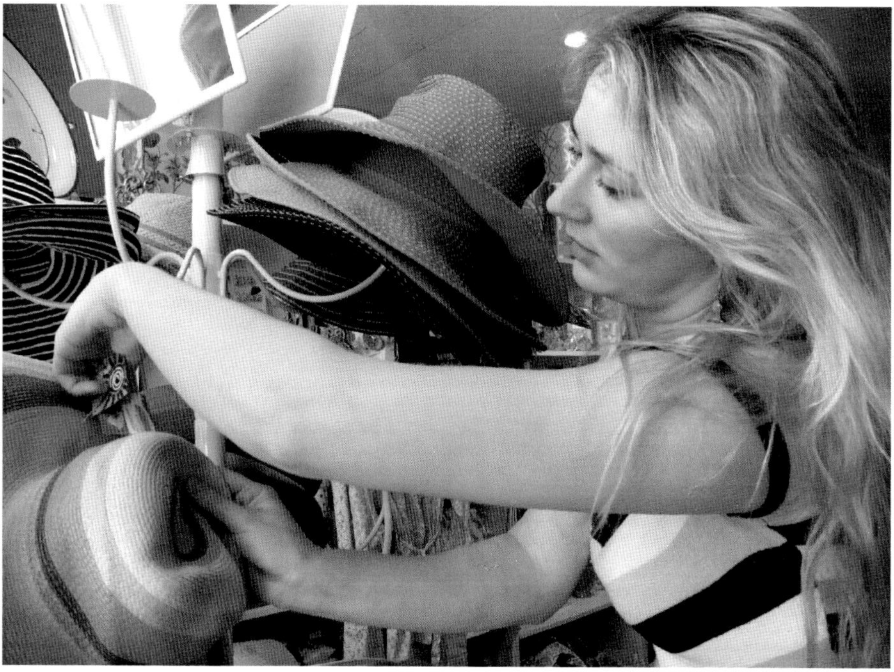

Mensura Kardasevic, a salesperson, at the Exchange's famous hat rack.

still appropriate." The compromises grew even more artful with the older girls: "They might want to wear black for the holidays. Well, lace can look a little—" Slutty—I say it for her. She grins. "Yeah. But taffeta can work."

In 2006, the Exchange began an immigrant training program, working with the International Institute to offer refugee women help with English language, job skills and cultural insights. Participants from poverty-stricken areas in Somalia and Honduras were first to complete the program. That same year, sales associate Maida Adilovic, a refugee from Bosnia, became a U.S. citizen.

In 2008, the Exchange celebrated its 125th anniversary. A grateful newsletter listed donors, among them names familiar in St. Louis philanthropic circles—Bush (William H.T. "Bucky" Bush, cousin to the president), Griesedieck, Orthwein, Barnes, Barksdale, Dubinsky, Knight, Metcalfe and scores more, including the Exchange's longtime landlord, Charles Cella.

A technical glitch was hurriedly fixed for the occasion: the website's address had begun "womansexchange"—and read as "woman sex change." It caused quite a few snorts of amusement, but it simply would not do as a permanent address. It was changed to woexstl.org.

The anniversary hoopla centered—no great surprise—on food and artful gifts. Melody Haffer had taken Bertha Cook's place overseeing the kitchen, and she and her team outdid themselves with menu additions: new soups (chicken corn chowder, creamy broccoli cheddar and chicken tortilla), take-out dinner entrées (from a delicate quiche Lorraine to a hearty, comforting meatloaf with macaroni and cheese) and homemade pies (blueberry cream and caramel apple). New lunch entrées had a light, contemporary touch: roasted eggplant with sliced tomato on toasted ciabatta, finished with fresh basil and balsamic vinaigrette; hummus and veggie wrap in a spinach tortilla; dilled egg salad and thin-sliced smoked salmon; roast beef with roasted red peppers, feta and fresh spinach on French bread; blanched asparagus and ham with a Parmesan/goat cheese spread; chicken breast with field greens, cucumber, red onion, tomato, shredded carrot, feta and a creamy lemon-dill dressing. The new salad tossed crisp field greens with dried cherries, goat cheese and glazed pecans.

And it was all served with toasted, buttered English muffins.

Consignors stayed busy for the anniversary. Linda Petersmeyer made a wide-eyed Susie doll, named in honor of long-serving children's chair Susie Sivewright. The doll's rose dress is appliquéd with pink cherries. Jo Ann, a widow who'd sewn for the Exchange for more than twenty years, created an exquisite bishop dress of white imperial broadcloth, its neckline hand smocked and embroidered with the signature cherries. Jewelry designer Diane Katzman created a limited-edition charm with the Exchange logo on one side and its foundation year, 1883, on the reverse. And customers were reminded of the heirloom-quality elbow-length gloves imported from Italy that could be monogrammed at the Exchange. After they'd been slid off in order to dine or dance, a lady's escort could confidently retrieve them and hand them to her without running the risk of stealing another woman's gloves in the process.

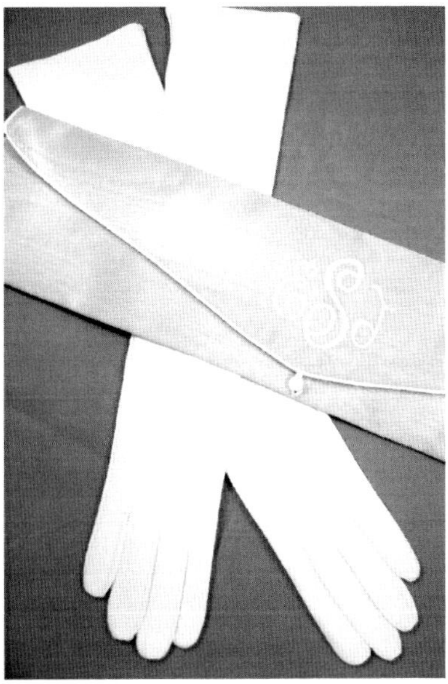

For more than a century, the Exchange has been monogramming gloves of soft Italian leather—one does not wish to pick up another lady's glove by mistake—and selling them in keepsake boxes. Special opera gloves were brought back for the anniversary at Becky Smith's suggestion. *Photo by Kyle Mallett.*

IN SEVENTH GRADE, Kelly Hoerr's friends had a slumber party for her thirteenth birthday, and they did the coolest thing they could think of. They each brought an ingredient and made the Woman's Exchange salad for dinner. (Somebody's mother bought the dressing from the Exchange.)

Flash forward to Hoerr, married and trying hard to get pregnant. She gets happy news from her obstetrician and then walks past the Woman's Exchange window and sees an antique white wicker bassinet overflowing with the softest, hand-stitched sheets. She buys the entire display.

Flash forward again, and she's the president, leading the Exchange through the 2010 recession. "We had some very slow months, and a few times where we decided we'd better not buy as much," she says. "That kind of thinking can be dangerous because if you don't have enough to sell…We had a lot of heated discussions about what kind of risks to take." By 2011, profits were rising again, and Hoerr was worrying about all the online opportunities for would-be consignors to sell their wares. The Exchange could try to sell more of its own inventory online, of course. "But the kind of quality we look for, you just can't see online," she sighs. You need to feel the fabric's softness, take in the eighth-inch bows and deep, perfect hems, have your little girl measured and measured again.

Jessica Wright's not the least bit scared of Etsy.com. "Those trends of making things at home and sourcing things locally are great for us," she says. She became the Exchange's executive director just as the pendulum took a wild swing back to handcraft. "Knitting's being reinvented, as knitters come up with

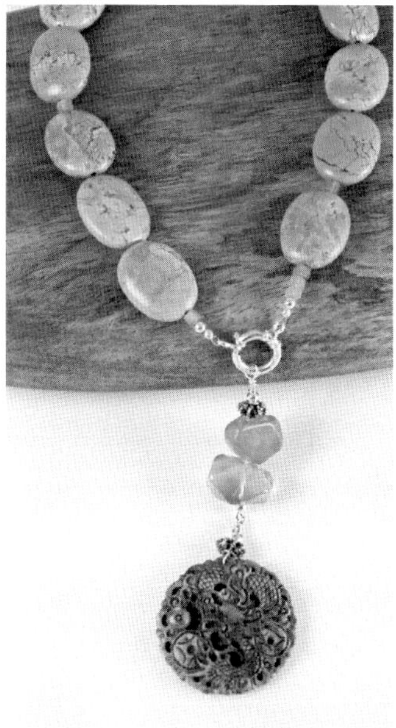

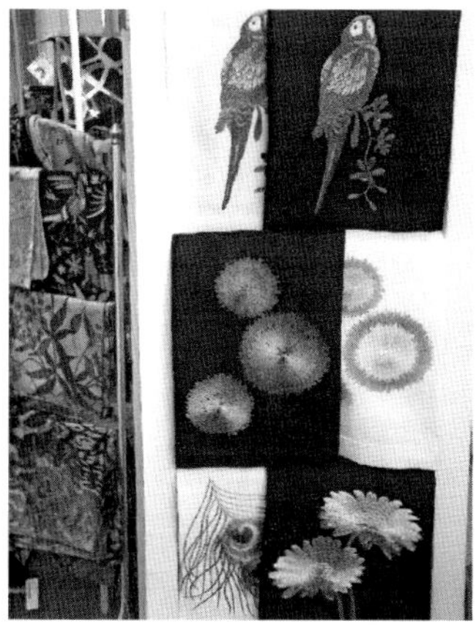

Top: The obligatory pearl choker has given way to jewelry inspired by other cultures, nature and abstract art. *Photo by Kyle Mallett.*

Bottom: These tea towels are as exquisitely embroidered as their Victorian counterparts—but far more vivid.

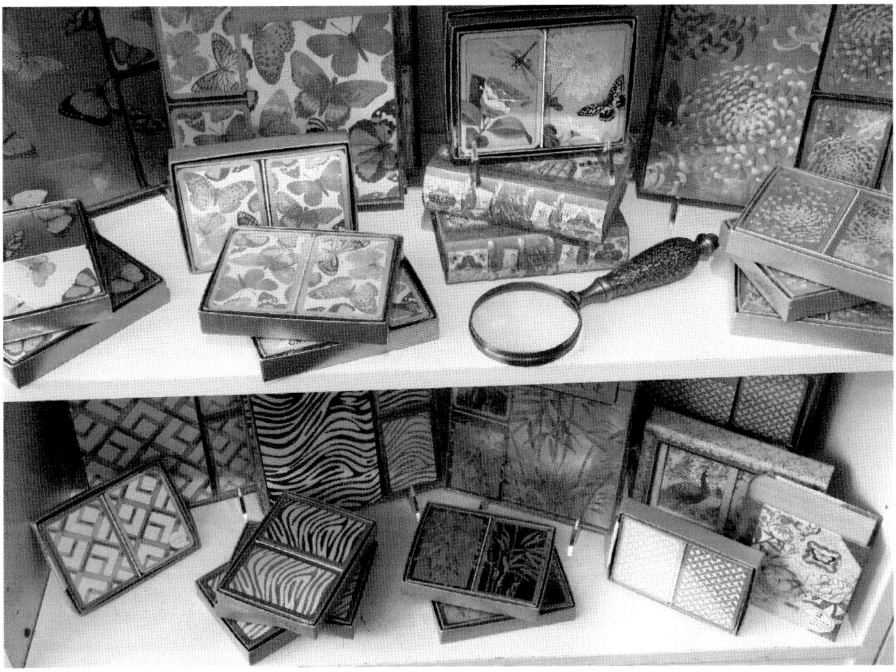

Bridge, like so much else in the Exchange's history, is back in style again.

new ideas for things they'd want to wear and buy," she says, "and more people are making jewelry. We've been doing all that for more than one hundred years."

She looks for local crafting organizations, collaboratives, nonprofits and art shows to partner with. "We can provide them with a bricks-and-mortar place for them to exhibit their work rather than having it just on the Internet. And we can give them some exposure in a neighborhood where they wouldn't otherwise be. We're finding we can go more contemporary here—we have gone a lot more contemporary since 2010, and our sales are up over 50 percent. Moms are always the same age, so they get younger all the time."

Customers still walk in dressed in preppie skirts, headbands and flats, "but more and more, they'll mix it up, maybe add a really cool, ethnic handbag, or unusual, arty earrings," Wright says. "The really cool, funky, different things are the first that sell." She stocks Mexican silk scarves sold only at one other boutique in the States, ceramics from Eva Gordon, fun hostess gifts like a bright red enameled tray with chrome trim and sharply angled sides and tongue-in-cheek dish glove and apron sets with faux mink trim. "The Exchange is Michael Aram's biggest account in Missouri," Wright points out, "and the shop was already selling the bone bracelets Oprah put on her 'Things I Love' list."

Custom's back, too, after a century in which machines and factories mass-produced everything. And since Wright arrived, the number of consignors, which was flagging, has almost doubled.

"It's not so much a challenge to find people who are talented and also in need," she explains. "It's more the fact that most of those people don't live or shop in Ladue. It's letting them know we are here to support them. The Internet helps tremendously—there's Etsy, and there are groups of smockers and seamstresses that communicate online. All consignors need to express to us, on a signed document, is that they need this income to support themselves and their family. We respect their dignity and their privacy." Always have.

Conclusion

The Art of Preservation

"Our clientele has changed," observed Edie Spink, lunching at her club in the last year of her life. She was ninety, and her ideas flew as fast as they did back in law school, or during her years as the longest-tenured mayor in Ladue. "Used to be, you were practically a member if you went there to eat," she mused. "But a whole new group of people has come in. Which is fine," she added hurriedly.

"It's actually good to get the word out about the Exchange," Janey Rouse pointed out. "It helps us get a larger repeat clientele. Our sales have gone up quite a bit, even in bad times."

"And we have men eating here!" Spink exclaimed.

In the early 1990s, when Joe Torre played baseball with the Cardinals, he often came into the tearoom with his wife. Every once in a while, a couple of guys brave the ruffles and come in for lunch, just because the food's so good. And ever since the Exchange started selling carryout dinners, bachelors and widowers in the neighborhood have been loyal, steady customers. But men know their place is on the periphery; the Exchange was built by women, for women, and it is anchored by domestic arts that have been largely relegated to women for centuries.

Ariadne wouldn't have minded seeing the men come in to shop and dine—but she might have felt dizzy at the pace of life, the struggle to find time to relax or plan a party or socialize. "Those lunches after working were great fun," Kary Matthews says. "Everything is so fast now, it's no longer an end unto itself, an opportunity to get away and be with other women.

Women have such full lives. If they take an afternoon off from the kids, they power-pack it with errands and the gym. There's a loss, I think."

Membership used to overlap, with mothers and daughters both on the board at the same time. That happens less often now; there are so many more options, so many competing ways to spend one's time.

The volunteer challenge remains a challenge.

Competition isn't just new shops in proximity anymore; it's online.

And for fundraising, competition is any charity with a shorter, clearer sound bite.

The Exchange's mission doesn't boil down to three words. It's relatively simple, but it's embedded in history, it's changed form over the years and it's easily misinterpreted as a group of sheltered, rich women playing Lady Bountiful for women with less luck and a stronger work ethic.

That's not the reality. The respect has been mutual. And board members have grown in independence and self-confidence just as surely as consignors have. There's tension, of course, just as there is between staff and board. You can hear it in the polite distance that enters their voices, the exasperation they're careful to hide, the amazed admiration they feel for one another's lives.

Financial stability is a constant goal for the Exchange, but that reality goes in cycles. "I remember crawling around the dusty attic in jeans with the treasurer, going through papers from the 1970s," Lewis says. "Thousands of pages of old financials—109 boxes over in cold storage in North St. Louis. Apparently, in the '70s, there was a financial crisis too."

Her solution to safeguard the future is to focus with even more determination on the mission, "really give more attention to our consignment and growing it beyond just children's into food and gift areas, jewelry, purses, immigrant training. I would love to get an endowment going—we've been talking about that since 2006—but right now we need every penny.

"Another anonymous gift would do it," she says suddenly, not willing to give up on the idea altogether. "And we need someone to coach us in fundraising—how do you ask for those 'transforming gifts'?" It's all a lot less personal than it was in 1883, when Ariadne made friends among the businessmen of St. Louis.

As the Exchange broadens its focus, it widens in a spiral, passing above its own history. The baked goods consignors brought in the late 1800s? Board member Lisa Cady brainstormed an idea with a friend, and now a program with St. Patrick's Center will bring spice mixes, rubs, beans-and-rice packets and barbecue sauces, all made in a certified commercial kitchen by aspiring

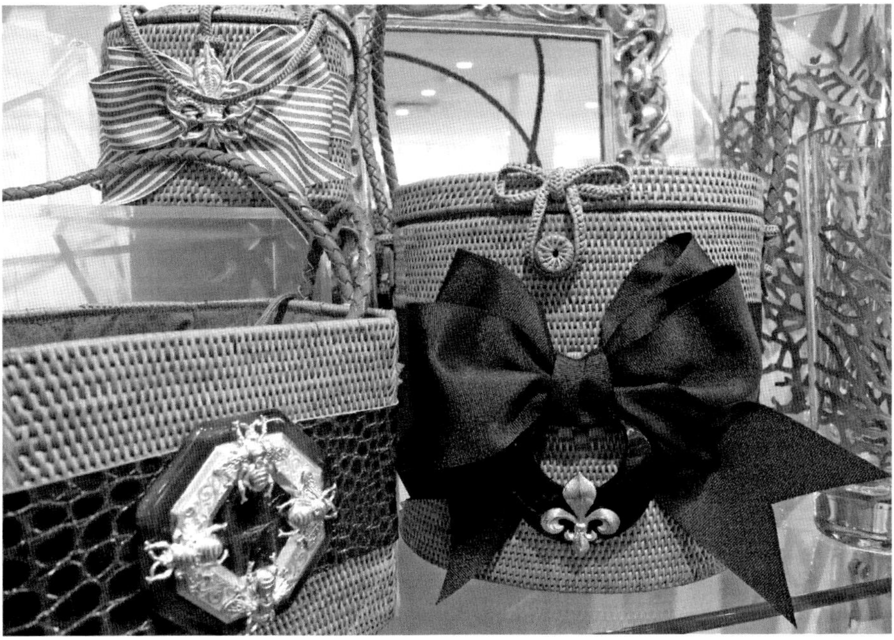

Buyers look for decorative details like these, which anchor a carefree, artful whimsy in classical tradition.

entrepreneurs, to the shelves of the Exchange. Cady says volunteers also hope to bring women into the tearoom kitchen at 4:00 a.m. to bake pastries and muffins, to "compete with Starbuck's" for the breakfast hour.

Hearing the plans, Matthews smiles. "We are coming full circle."

THE ST. LOUIS EXCHANGE never once dreamed of closing; the need always seemed too pressing. Richmond's Exchange, however, closed back in 1955, Milwaukee's in 1965 and Cincinnati's in 1985, after 102 years in business. By the time Sharon Bean became president of the National Federation of Woman's Exchanges in 2001, the St. Louis Woman's Exchange was one of the oldest in the country.

There are now nineteen Exchanges across the country. One closed in 2010 (the Sassy Cat, in Chagrin Falls, Ohio), but one opened in 2010: the Women's Gift Exchange of Grayson County, in Texas. Another group, in Lexington, Kentucky, formed in 2011 to sell crafts made by women overseas. A group in Utah—farther west than any Woman's Exchange in American history—started talking in 2011, too.

"For years, we all looked at each other and said, 'Application for membership? We've been losing members!'" Lewis recalls. "But now we need that application!" Times are tough economically, so a volunteer-based not-for-profit organization selling handcrafted merchandise seems smart again.

Provided the skills can be resurrected.

When the St. Louis Exchange was founded, virtually every woman knew how to sew and embroider, even if she snarled the thread a bit or made lumpy stitches. Today, virtually no one knows how to hem a skirt, let alone serge and smock. The Exchange's mission hasn't changed—it's still helping women support themselves with creativity, dignity, discipline and refined skill. But a new purpose has been added. By showcasing its consignors' work, the Exchange helps preserve and encourage these arts. Even the tearoom and gift shop do a bit of preservation by insisting on enduring quality, excellent taste and civilized, convivial relationships.

Patterns run through the past thirteen decades: A constant balancing of quality with thrift. Revenue zigzagging like rick-rack. Redecorating a regular motif. And the running thread, an almost daily discernment of what to keep and when to change. American culture urges people to keep up, keep up—yet one can sometimes have more success by staying with the old ways.

December 18, 2013, marks the 130th anniversary of the St. Louis Woman's Exchange.

Ann Scott smiles, remembering all the times of panic. "Every time a store opened close to us, everybody was ready to slit their wrists. But it never mattered. Then everybody said, 'Oh, we need to sell more blue jeans, be more trendy.' But we didn't." As it turned out, customers were relieved to have a sanctuary from fleeting fads and disposable chic. They knew what they bought at the Exchange would be finely made, and its charm would never turn to kitsch.

"St. Louis is a small town, a close-knit circle," Matthews points out. "It's very southern. People come into the Woman's Exchange as members—either they're pulled dragging and screaming by their mothers, or they come willingly with their friends. As long as St. Louis remains that kind of place, with an extended social circle—and I don't mean social in the uppity sense but in the sense of human communion—there will continue to be an energetic, enthusiastic driving force. There will always be a need for the kind of help we have been able to give."

Will there always be a market? Nobody puts their sons in sailor suits anymore, and nobody knows how to iron puffed sleeves and sashes. "The

The Exchange is far too well mannered to dish about celebrity buyers. But in the early years of the last century, it's said, a little boy named Vincent Price—five years old and already a terror—was buttoned into one of the Exchange's Peter Thompson sailor suits. (If the experience traumatized him, future audiences benefited.) In this century, Gwyneth Paltrow is said to have ordered a cherry dress for Apple, just as Jacqueline Kennedy did decades earlier for Caroline, with a matching boy's outfit for John-John. The March 2010 *Traditional Home* pictured designer Alessandra Branca's daughters in cherry dresses.

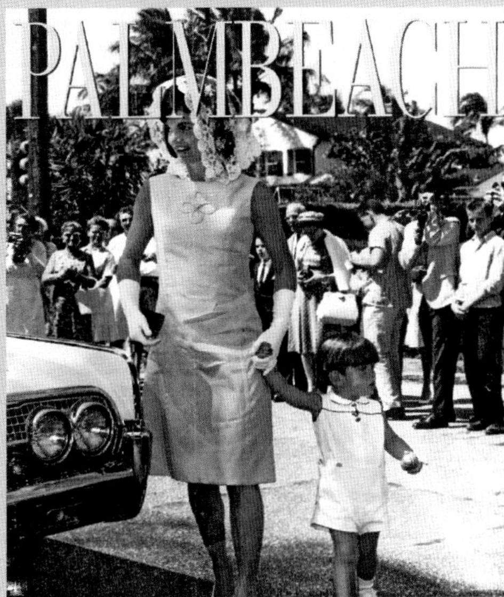

First Lady Jacqueline Kennedy dressed her children in cherry finery from the St. Louis Woman's Exchange.

Peter Pan collar has gone the way of Peter Pan," Matthews sighs. "But the cherry dress never changes—they are teaching new consignors, thank God. And if we could find another woman who would do the beautiful embroidery for those fairy-tale dresses, people would pay a fortune. The faster we go, the more we will want to hold on to the finer points of our past. The more we change jobs, the more we will appreciate the old crafts and fine goods. They have a long shelf-life, and they pack away beautifully for the next generation, and the next and the next. The Gap stuff is really cute for ten minutes, and then you throw it in the wash and it falls apart.

"Good taste never goes away."

Appendix A

Consignors

The Cherry Dress Maker

Ellie Dressel has spent the past twenty-six years making the most famous dress in St. Louis. Two little girls wore it to present flowers to the queen of England. Jacqueline Kennedy dressed John-John in its little boy counterpart, the cherry button suit. Gwyneth Paltrow ordered a cherry dress for Apple.

Dressel doesn't pay much attention to the celebrity factor. She says she saw a little girl wearing her dress in public only once, at the Muny summer theater. "But then, I don't travel in those circles," she adds with a grin.

For Dressel, the dress meant a chance to stay home and watch over her son, who had cognitive disabilities. She became a consignor in 1973, when he started school.

"It took me a long time to get the confidence to purchase fabric, knowing that I probably wouldn't get paid for it for a couple months," she remembers. "I had a sewing machine, but I didn't have a lot of fabric that was appropriate. Little by little, I gained the confidence to give it a whirl."

She'd been sewing steadily for the Exchange for thirteen years—bibs, blankets, whatever was needed—when one of the members asked if she'd like to make the famous cherry dress. "The woman making it was in her seventies, and her brother was dying," Dressel remembers. "But she wouldn't give me her pattern! They gave me a dress—I couldn't cut it apart, but I could see how it was made."

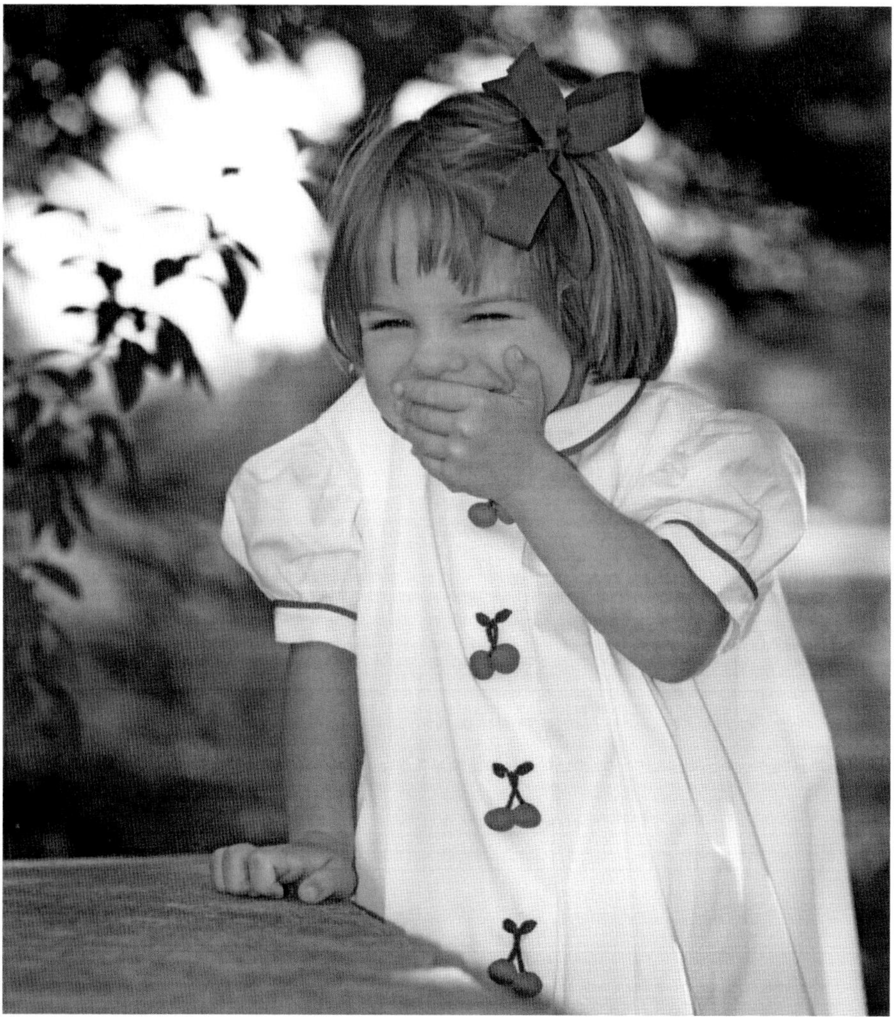

Hadley Jones Key, age four, wearing her cherry dress to Ladue Chapel Nursery School. *Courtesy of Richard Benkof Photography.*

The original dress was white, with box pleats, a Peter-Pan collar piped in red and four pairs of cherries that dangled merrily down the center front. Dressel practiced those cherries for hours, cutting circles of red fabric, rolling their edges under, stuffing them, pulling them tightly closed and crocheting stems to sew into them. She now makes the dress in many different colors. She works in batches of four or five dresses, one color at a time, so she doesn't have to change thread. "I'll do four pink collars, then four pink sleeves." By year's end, she's often made an orchard full, sometimes as many as 450 or 500, many of them ordered from out of state and a handful from Europe.

Dressel's sewing room takes up half her basement, and her machines are set along an L-shaped table. "If I'm serging something, finishing the seams, I can just turn around and roll a couple feet to the sewing machine," she explains. "And of course my ironing board lives up!" She loves the substance and smoothness of the high-end fabrics the Exchange requires. "It's like the difference in quilt fabric. You can get it at Walmart, and it might be the same print, but it's different fabric—you can practically see through some of it. The more threads to the inch, the finer your fabric is." Over the years, she's perfected her finishing: "I like my things to look as nice on the inside as on the outside."

As off-the-rack clothes became shoddier, Dressel's have continued unchanged, their quality and fine detailing irreproachable. Dressel still crochets each cherry stem with delicate precision; she still leaves the three-inch hems that can be let out as little girls grow. When Guy Trebay wrote about the cherry dress for the *New York Times* in 2007, St. Louis native Carrie Polk told him, "Three generations in our family have worn them. They're like clothes from before the disposable-clothes era, with hems the size of Texas. You didn't just spill chocolate on one and pitch it. You got it cleaned and ironed, and if you grew, you brought down the hem."

Dressel's dresses might span generations, but her craftsmanship does not. She couldn't even interest her own daughters in learning. "Garment sewing is just not a thing many people do anymore," she says. "They don't care about the pride in making something yourself; they think it's easier to go buy it. I had a young woman say to me, 'You can buy such cute things—why would you want homemade?' And that's the difference. I see handmade; she sees homemade."

The Bookworm and the Tutu-Maker

Kathey Craft's mother refused to teach her to sew. "She just set me loose and let me use her machine," Craft says, "and by the time I was sixteen, I was making her clothes." In 1988, Craft saw an article in the *St. Louis Post-Dispatch* about the Woman's Exchange. "It was two years it took me to get up enough nerve to make a sample for them," she says. "In 1990, I did it. I made a long-waisted, filmy white dress with a double skirt, and a blue

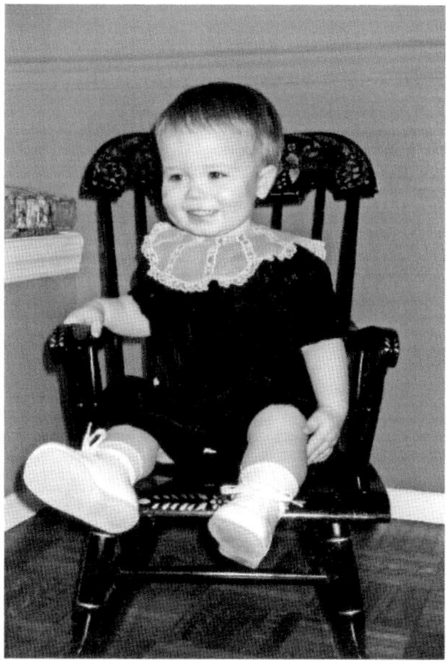

Blackmail for a future CEO.

ribbon around the hips and embroidery down the V-neck. I sweated bullets over that dress."

The manager examined the French seams and said, "Well, you certainly know your way around a sewing machine."

"What does that mean?" Craft asked herself.

The manager said, "We'll be in touch." Craft smiled uncertainly and went home.

Two weeks later, the orders started to arrive.

She loved, still loves, the satisfaction of turning bits of thread and fabric into a finished, perfect garment. "You are just kind of singing your song to the Creator," she says. "Now, there are days when it's not like that. Like the tutus. I could not get them right, and I kept sending them back, and the Exchange would send more fabric and finally my mom couldn't stand it anymore." Helen Bailey gathered up the netting and made the perfect tutu, and from that moment on, she was the Exchange's tutu maker. Now eighty, she's still hard at work. "She tried to tell some lady how to do it one time," Craft says, "and we never heard from her again. Net is very difficult to work with. I watch her, though, because you never know when you're going to be called into service."

One of Craft's first projects for the Exchange, more than twenty years ago, was "this black velvet bubble, for a baby. It had a removable French collar of white organdy and lace, and tabs on the front with two big white pearl buttons. All in one piece. Mrs. Busch [of the famous brewery family] wanted one for her baby boy, and she wanted blue velvet. Not velveteen, thick velvet, and the collar she wanted tea dyed. We were just a couple of bumpkins from the South Side, and we looked at that order and said, 'No way!' So we actually turned down work from the rich and famous. You have to be honest. Material's expensive, and you don't want to mess it up. Although if you do mess it up, they won't say a word. They'll just keep sending you more fabric."

Mother and daughter moved to Prospect, Tennessee, a few years ago, but the Exchange wasn't about to let them quit. "No problem," the manager said, "we'll just ship you fabric, and you ship back the items." They don't have space for a workroom inside their trailer, so they share a small building behind it. "It's got a cutting table in the middle, and one side's mine, and one side's hers," Craft says. "I've got my serger and my sewing machine in the back corner, and pegboard all along the back, and I've got all my thread up there—it looks pretty. And I have bookcases, because I'm famous for my ponderous collection of books."

Years ago, Craft did quit sewing for the Exchange to take a job at a casino. Then, when her kids seemed old enough to handle it, she divorced. Soon after, she suffered a heart attack.

"I couldn't get out of bed in the morning," she says. "I couldn't hold a job. I was living on $530 a month, and I had two daughters at home." She lay there, sick with dread, until she got enough energy to start worrying about what she was going to do. With sudden clarity, she remembered the Exchange and wondered if she could go back.

"Can you come out today?" Jacque Thieme asked her. When Craft arrived, Thieme said, "Take Kathey up and give her all the work she wants."

"I felt like I had just died and went to heaven," Craft says. "I went home with all this fabric. They use a good quality fabric, an Imperial broadcloth. It's real smooth, and it has a good body. You get used to that feel." She talks happily about smocking and bibs, Victorian white work and heirloom sewing. Then she falls silent.

"No one expects to have illness punctuate their life like it has mine," she says. "If it weren't for the Exchange, I don't know what would have happened to me."

Gathering a Thousand Pictures

Rita Cozadd started smocking thirty years ago, when her daughter was a baby. Cozadd saw a tiny, exquisitely smocked dress and fell in love with it but couldn't afford to buy it. "I finally got the name of the lady who made it, and she gave me a few patterns and I came home and taught myself," she says. "Now I've got over one thousand designs, so I make whatever strikes my fancy."

In the beginning, she used iron-on dots to mark the fabric. "You had to go in and out with a needle to make your pleats, before you even started smocking," she says. "Then I heard of a 'pleater'—it was made in South Africa. I figured it had to be easier. It has needles and four brass rods. You

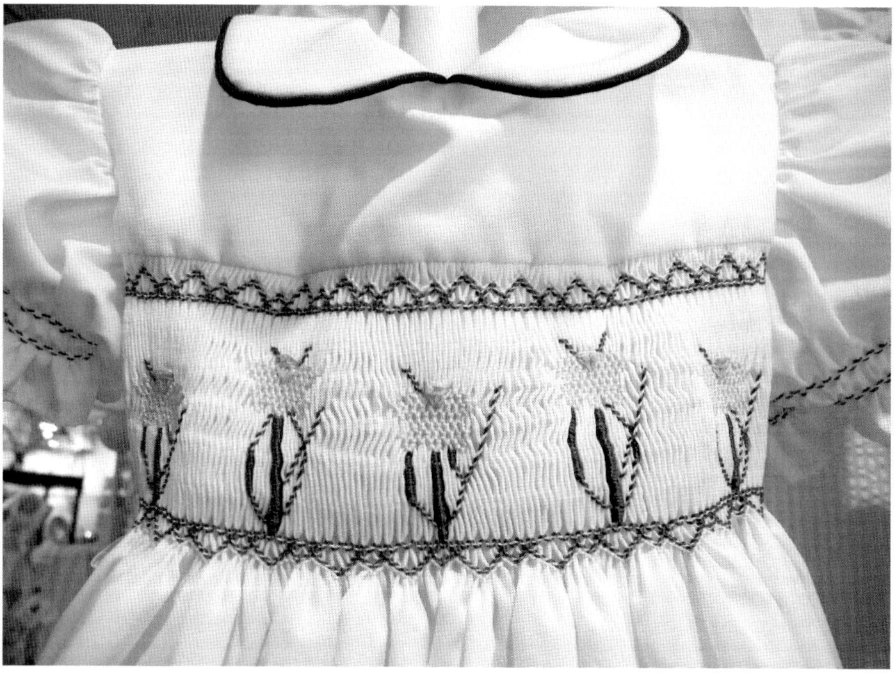

Not many people know how to smock like this anymore.

gather your forty-five-inch fabric up to about ten inches across, using the pleater, and then you start your embroidery stitching—usually chain and cable stitches—right across those pleats. Your basting thread and your pleats form a graph, and you just work your pattern, changing colors. I've got patterns for Snow White, Cinderella, just about anything you can think of."

She started working for the Exchange when one of its members saw her dresses at a craft show. "I have a special-needs foster child; she's been with us nineteen years," Cozadd explains. "To work out[side] of the house—I really can't." She quickly learned the Exchange's color strategy: "Yellow on infants tends to make them look jaundiced. And mint green just doesn't sell. They generally don't have a lot of purple, either. They like pink, and a brighter spring green." The women at the Exchange might be particular, but they are easy to work with, she adds. "They're more than happy to teach me new techniques, and anything you might need that's not available in town, you can buy through them."

Cozadd set up her workroom carefully: two long tables to hold her embroidery machine, serger and sewing machine and then rolling carts with zippers, threads and buttons. "A friend's going to build me fabric racks, like at the store," she says happily. She's also started burning scented soy candles for herself while she works—apple cinnamon and, at Christmastime, pine.

The classic designs that stay in constant demand, Cozadd can smock in about five hours. New designs take far longer. And then there's cutting out the pattern pieces, assembling the dress.

"Now I'm wanting to learn shadow embroidery," she confides. "It's beautiful. You use an organza, and you stitch underneath and form a picture that shows through. "I've always wanted to learn tatting, too. It's a lost art—you can't find many people who know anything about it."

What about smocking—will that soon be a lost art, too?

"Oh, I don't think so. I've got my one daughter smocking—she does beautiful picture smocking. I think it will continue. You don't find that quality of workmanship anywhere else. And there are enough people who love it."

First Comes the Little Branch...

Patricia Degenhart used to lunch with friends at the Exchange. Sometimes she'd notice their ads in her needlework magazines, advertising handmade infants' and children's clothing. She thought nothing of it—until a decade ago, when her husband was diagnosed with cancer. "I just panicked," she says, a little of that wild fear coming back into her voice as she remembers. "I went over to the Exchange and showed them sweaters I had made. One was an owl cardigan—it's an ancient pattern, probably conceived in the '40s."

They loved it and ordered more. And more.

"It certainly helped me through a rough emotional time," she says now. "My husband passed away in 2009, and people from the Exchange sent so many cards and letters. You get acquainted with these people, you say little things as you take in your garments, and you become comfortable with one another."

As for her famous sweater, "it has two owls, about two and a half inches high, and their little feet are standing on a branch," she says. "On the back, there are four more owls. They sell in pink, light blue, white, red and navy. One time I had a special order for a little white owl, white on white, and Maureen [Wagner, a longtime salesperson] read me this note the recipient had written about how much she enjoyed it and was proud of the little sweater. I was over the moon!"

She likes to knit all kinds of sweaters, she says, sounding a little wistful. "They're intent on getting that owl sweater! They will sell every single one I can make." She mastered its knits and purls and cable twists long ago: "I know when the owls start and finish. First comes the little branch, and you do a right and left twist to make the little feet and another for the head."

She no longer even misses the wools she used to use: "The young mother nowadays is more interested in acrylic or cotton than even washable wool—I think it scares them. It's more work. You often need to wash it by hand, and you can't put it in the dryer. When you have babies, every moment counts."

She finishes one tiny, perfect sweater every two weeks. "I like baby stuff," she says, her voice tender. "And it's a project that's easy to carry around." She pauses. "Not only does this work give you a source of income, it also gives you a lot of self-esteem," she says softly. "I don't think I'm the only one that needs it."

Making It Personal

Carol Schrick took sewing for four years straight at Cleveland High School, all the way up to custom tailoring. She was selling her handmade clothing at craft fairs when someone told her about the Exchange. "I was going through a divorce, and they were so supportive," she remembers. "I don't know what I would have done without the Exchange. They actually provided me with a brand-new sewing machine. They told me I could work as much as I wanted. They actually, at one point, gave me 100 percent commission, until I got on my feet again."

A quarter-century later, her children grown and happy, Schrick's still sewing eight or ten hours a day, four or five days a week. She specializes in custom machine embroidery, personalizing garments for special occasions. She embroiders names on cupcakes for birthdays, embroiders names and adds cherries, embroiders nursery

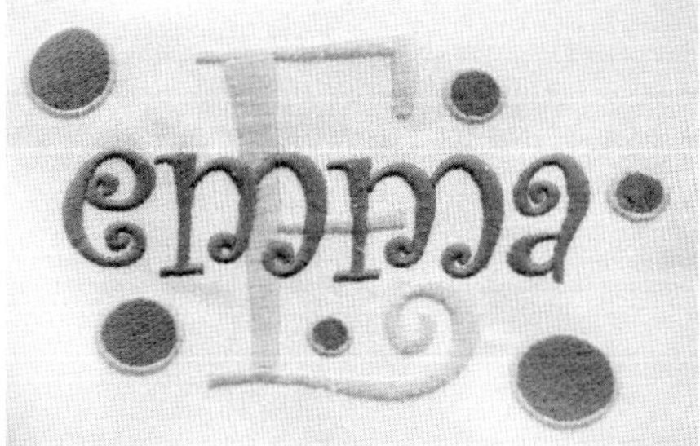

For a little girl, a monogram makes a dress important and special.

rhyme characters or skaters on a pond or tiny villages for Christmas. "The Exchange provides me with whatever fabric I need," she says. "Their colors used to be all pastel, but they've gotten a little brighter, which I like. I think they are starting to cater to younger buyers.

"I start Christmas clothes and towels in June," she says. "For birthdays, I'll do anything. One lady wanted a circus theme, so I made a circus train with animals. Another lady wanted something with monkeys. I like being able to create my own designs."

The Year of the Clowns

Linda Petersmeyer worked for a bank before her first child was born, but after her second child, she needed a job she could do from home. As a trial, the Exchange gave her a horse, a cat and a dog and told her to make one of each. Her samples were such a success that she went home, sat down at her sewing machine and burst into tears.

"What on earth is wrong?" her husband asked.

"They ordered two dozen of each!" she sobbed. "I'll never get it done in my whole life! I'll be here forever!"

With each toy she finished, she felt calmer. Soon, the Exchange made her its official doll maker. "They are all cloth dolls, all made from scratch, with hand-embroidered faces," she says. "And I make the big dancing dolls. They come as high as a grown-up's waist, and they hook onto the child's feet, and she dances with them.

"I name all my dolls," she adds, "because that way, when someone orders, we're not going through 'the one with the pigtails' or 'the one with braids on top of her head.'" For the Exchange's 125th anniversary, she made Susie, blond-haired and blue-eyed, all innocence, clad in a raspberry pink puffed-sleeve dress adorned with lighter pink cherries.

"I also make a lot of the clothes for, well, an eighteen-inch doll, and they happen to fit the American Girl doll," Petersmeyer says. She makes tiny holiday dresses, red-and-green plaid with solid bodices and puffy sleeves, and for Halloween, she makes witch and Dorothy costumes. She also does appliqué work and stitches cherries, butterflies, flowers and hearts on the seats of babies' little panties. And she makes everything for the Christmas window displays.

Except in the year of the clowns.

"I designed a clown," she explains. "When I first took it in, they said, 'Oh, we're not sure, but we'll try it.'" Orders poured in. "I was getting something like thirty-six orders a day. They had to buy stuff for the Christmas windows that year."

The clown is made of soft-sculpture fabric, and it's huge. "We did the big clowns for a long time, and then all of a sudden, the manager said, 'Why don't you make a little one?' and oh my gosh, there we went again with the orders."

Once the clowns were under control, Petersmeyer went back to making the annual window display as well. One year, she made a life-sized Santa and Mrs. Claus. "Mrs. Santa wore a size twenty-two dress," she recalls. "I'd laid her on one twin bed and Mr. Santa on the other, so I could stuff them." Finished, she went back to her workroom to tackle a different project. Then she heard one of the guys putting siding on her house yell, "Hey, come here. You won't believe this!"

Just as Petersmeyer's kids reached their teens, her husband died—young, unexpectedly—and her sewing became their only income. "One time, I didn't have much work, and I asked if there was anything else I could do, and Jacque Thieme, the manager, said, 'You know, anything we put in the windows sells.' She put all my dancing dolls in the window, and oh my gosh, they went."

She smiles, remembering. Then her voice changes. "The day my husband died, I'd been by the shop that morning. I came home and found him dead of a massive heart attack. One of the first people who walked in the funeral home was Jacque."

Why Sell a Monkey Naked?

When Linda Petersmeyer had more orders for dolls than a workshop of elves could have handled, she pulled her friend Brenda Thrasher out of retirement to help.

"I'd always sewn, but I'd never made money on it," Thrasher says. "I usually just made things for people." Soon after she started getting paid for her doll making, another consignor tired of making baby quilts and offered her the patterns—which was a bit like a sculptor offering the mold for her finest casting. Thrasher took the patterns with alacrity and started stitching: elephants with balloons, rabbits with balloons, bears with balloons.

"I make them in pastels, and they also like the elephant in a bright red," she says. "The character's on a center of white, then there's a six-inch trim of gingham in the same color, then a six-inch border of white where I put points," fabric double-folded into narrow triangles, "in the same color as the character."

Thrasher spends at least three days making the basic quilt. Then she machine embroiders the characters with a satin stitch and spends five long evenings doing the actual quilting. She refuses to use the usual two- or four-ounce batting; hers is eight ounces, which makes for a fluffier quilt that won't flatten anytime soon. "They've never complained," she says, eyes twinkling. "I also make a six-inch-square quilt with the baby's name and date of birth. They call it the Newman Quilt because Mr. Newman of Brown Shoe Co. wanted them made whenever his employees had a baby. Now all sorts of people ask for 'em."

In her first years, Thrasher embroidered all those babies' names by hand. "Then I got myself an embroidery machine," she says smugly. "Puttin' all that on there in satin stitch, that's kind of tough. And with the machine, it looks a lot neater." She also makes three-piece sets, satin-stitching bunnies on a hoodie, washcloth and towel. "And I make monkeys," she chortles. "They

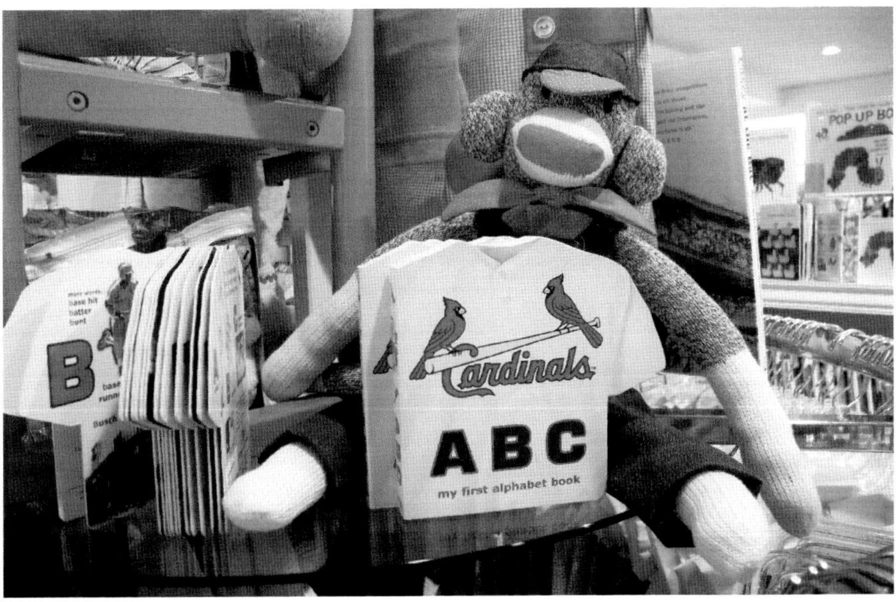

Might as well make the sock monkeys gray; when they were blue, children carried them around so diligently that they *turned* gray!

sometimes sell 'em naked, but I put an outfit on them: denim overalls with a dotted-Swiss hankie in the pocket, a dotted-Swiss neck scarf and a ball cap."

The monkeys are the most fun to make, Thrasher says. "You start with a pair of gray tube socks, and the body is one sock, with the legs coming from the ribbed part and the arms, ears, mouth and tail made out of the other sock." Her quilts require a bit more care. "You're sitting there quilting, and you look down and see a spot where one of your kids went by with sticky fingers! Oh, and once, I put a quilt together, and I was ironing it, ready to take it to the Exchange, and I looked down and I'd missed the material on part of my satin stitching. The ass of the elephant! I had to take out all that stitching and start over."

She's often awed by the other consignors' work. "There's an awful lot of talent at the Woman's Exchange," she says. "Some of the clothes they make, I wish I knew how to do it. I remember back in the old days, my mom could do that smocking, but she never did show me how. I'm really sad that she didn't. And now my kids aren't interested in hand quilting at all."

A devil's advocate question: is anything really lost in the switch to cheaper, faster mass production? "We are losing tradition. I remember my grandma making quilts. She was from Germany, and she tied hers; that's how they did it. And it was my mother-in-law who taught me to hand quilt. Even sewing—it's hard finding material, and they don't teach it in home ec anymore. We used to have to make our outfits, and we'd have a fashion show. I understand the reasoning. You can walk into a store and buy clothes faster."

She's silent a moment.

"But it's not quite the same."

BRINGING TOYS TO LIFE

Twenty years ago, Pauline Schroer solemnly carried several of her finest teddy bears into the Woman's Exchange and presented them for inspection. The bears passed muster, and Shroer was given several dolls that she could take apart to make patterns. For her favorite, Raggedy Ann, she already had a pattern. And when a grandmother requested a Raggedy Ann with gray hair and bifocals, Schroer burst out laughing. "No problem. I look in the mirror and see that every morning!"

She devises Christmas tree skirts without a pattern at all. One year, she layered red felt onto white satin and created a poinsettia. Another year, she made giant ABC blocks and two-foot crayons for the September window

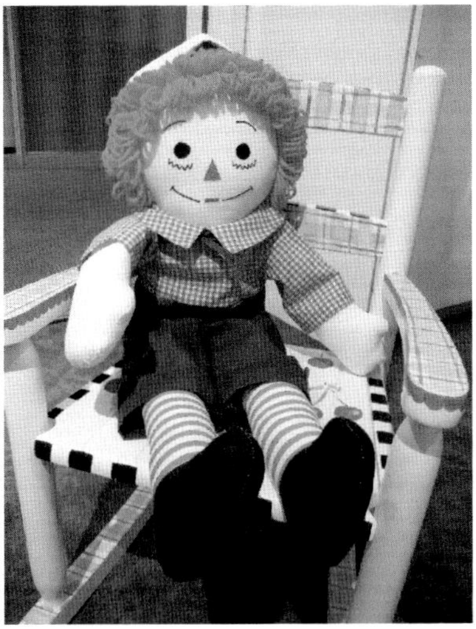

Raggedy Andy has taken myriad forms over the years, but he's always recognizable. His rocker is, of course, hand-painted.

display. "It's nice to have something to do," she says. "I worked twenty-nine years as a doctor's assistant. I'm seventy-three now, and I have some back problems, so I can't just go find a job. But I can't sit and do nothing." She also makes little gingham ponies, and Humpty Dumpties of various sizes and a pillow with a doll nestled inside so a little girl can carry her baby doll in comfort.

"You have no idea what goes into making some of these dolls," Schroer remarks. "We buy the stuffing in twenty-five-pound bags from Batesville, Arkansas. The bag is about five feet tall—I can barely get my arms around it—and once you split that bag open, it balloons. You would be amazed how much stuffing is in those dolls. You just stuff and stuff and stuff until it is so tight, and if you have to pull it back out, you think, 'How did I get all that in there?'"

Schroer's favorite toy to make is the Embroidered Bunny, which she says in a capital-letter way, like she's reading *Winnie-the-Pooh*. "You put it together like a quilt, thirty-five pieces, and as you put it together, you embroider on it, section by section," she explains. "It takes a little while—you don't make one of those bunnies overnight. But the Exchange doesn't rush you on anything unless it's really, really important.

"I do enjoy seeing them after they're done," she admits. "You get three or four of them sitting around, and they just look like they're talking to you." It's the same with the baby sock monkeys, although making them can be maddening: "You're trying to cut the ears out of this teeny sock, and there's no room to do anything. But after you get four or five done, you look up, and there are these little baby monkeys sitting there looking back at you!"

Stitching a Life

Zareen Razawi came to the United States as a refugee back in 2001. Her husband was still in Afghanistan; she'd come ahead with their three children.

"I went first to Maine, for a month, and from Maine to here I took four buses with three kids and my suitcases," she says. "I don't think I'm going to forget in my whole life. The kids were crying, and I was so scared. I didn't know a.m. and p.m.—when I saw on my ticket it was 4:00 p.m., I was thinking in the middle of the night. And I was asking people, and they didn't understand me. I wanted to know if I missed my stop, and they didn't understand."

In 2002, her English as a second language teacher, Cathy Ross, asked about her life in Afghanistan. "I told her I sewed, and she gave me information about the Woman's Exchange. We went together—in the beginning, I didn't drive."

As samples, she brought simple gray broadcloth pajamas she'd made for her little boy, stitching them with care. "I didn't have a good machine over there, but it was looking good. And for my daughter, what I brought was a little bit fancy, a full blue skirt with a very shiny, light blue ribbon around the hem. I made it for her when she was six."

The women at the Exchange complimented her work, and she just nodded, unable to form a full response in English but thinking how nice they were. "I was feeling so good that I went there," she says. "I was getting a feeling that it was a good place to just work with them."

She's done so ever since, moving from simple blankets and towels to elaborate pleated dresses that have to be measured and marked perfectly or they won't hang properly.

In the early years, she didn't drive, so the Exchange sometimes mailed her the fabric to make it easier. "They didn't rush me; they gave me plenty of time. As long as it got back to them correct." One of her friends tried to sew for the Exchange, she says, "but she did some things that were wrong, and she got tired of the simple things. I said, 'It should be perfect and clean, because it's important.' Some people, they are thinking, 'It's inside of the dress; it doesn't matter.' But I'm not that kind of person."

She made a catastrophic mistake only once. She didn't know corduroy had to be cut with all the pieces going in the same direction or it would pick up the light differently. "When it's upside down, the color is changing," she says, wincing. "I was saving the fabric, wondering why they'd given me so much extra. Then I am looking at it, and it is a different color. I took all the dresses to them. They called me and told me, 'This is wrong,' but they didn't make me do them over, and they paid me for the dresses also. I didn't understand words on the phone very easily, but a friend who worked at Eunice Farmer Fabrics [Susan Rozmarin] showed me what I did wrong and how to cut it out so it wouldn't happen again. I thought they would send me back all those dresses so I could fix them, and I didn't mind, but they just said, 'It's OK this time.'"

She never misjudged corduroy again. Five years ago, Razawi's husband joined her in St. Louis. Now they have a fourth child, a toddler, and Razawi is thrilled that she can work from home.

"I learned to sew from my brother," she says. "In the stores in Afghanistan, it is all men who sew. Women sew in the house."

Here, she sews for the Exchange.

Surprised by Life

Jacque Thieme's five children were nearly grown when, at the age of forty, she had a surprise baby. Little Heather was pure delight—until Thieme's husband became ill, and she had to find a way to support them. "I knew I could sew," she says, "because I had made wedding gowns for Heather's three older sisters. When I was pregnant with her, I had to go find, would you believe, a mother-of-the-bride maternity dress!" She wasn't sure, though, how to find work sewing. Then one of her older daughters' friends saw a tiny dress Thieme had made for Heather and said, "You have got to take this to the Woman's Exchange!" The girl knew all about the Exchange, it turned out, because her mother was on the board.

Thieme took the advice—and the Exchange took the dress on the spot. "They asked how many more I would make!" She was thrilled. She sewed for five years, then joined the shop staff and then became manager. The women at the Exchange were the village she needed to raise her daughter without her husband's help. When she had to find an apartment, Laurie Selkirk took her down to the Selkirk auction house and bought her furniture. Janey Rouse brought in treasures she insisted she was "clearing out," saving Thieme's pride.

"So it was easy for me to love the Exchange even more," Thieme says now. "Most people would never dream what these women do behind the scenes. They just see their pictures at galas."

Thieme's youngest daughter grew up with Exchange board members watching over her like a row of seraphim. "These women managed to be there at every important juncture in her life and even helped her apply to universities," Thieme recalls. "She used to say, "Mom, I feel like I have one hundred mothers!"

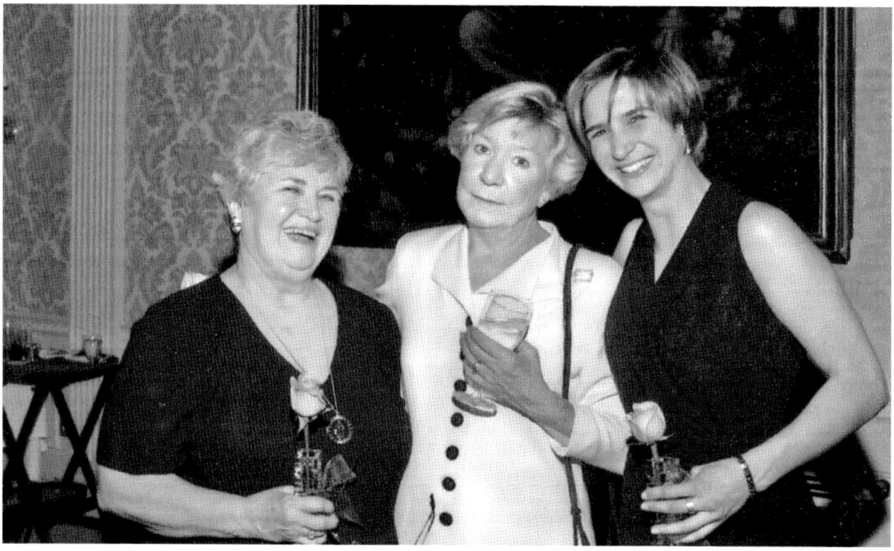

Jacque Thieme, Laurie Selkirk and Heather Thieme, who grew up with "one hundred mothers" at the Exchange.

Thieme enjoyed even the hassles of her job—stalking potential thieves, washing dishes when the dishwasher quit and staying until 11:00 p.m. to turn the shop into a Christmas fairyland. She especially loved the shopping trips in New York—but the board members' audacity terrified her. "Barbara Roberts and Penny Rogers and I would go to New York to the fabric houses, and then we would go up and down Madison Avenue, in and out of every children's store, searching for ideas. One time, Penny and I were in this shop, and Penny whips out her camera, and I'm having a nervous breakdown saying, 'Oh my God, you can't take a picture!' The woman came over and said, 'I would like you to leave my store right now!'" Thieme was trembling. "I am the world's greatest coward. They had a lot more courage. Another time they bought this little book—they said, 'Our friend Jacque is going to be a grandmother'—they made all this up!—'and we wanted to just buy this book for her.' They made the owner write in the book for me, 'Dear Jacque…' They were buying time to look around!

"Those gals were great at bluffing their way in," she continues, grinning. "Once, we wanted this wonderful tartan plaid, and you had to buy thousands of yards to be a customer. We'd go in, and they would tell their story and talk these men into saying, 'OK, you can buy only so many bolts.' We made little plaid skirts for girls, with straps that went over the shoulder and crisscrossed in back. And we bought beautiful lawn fabric from England.

"Some of the New York stores were awful," she remarks. "Millions of bolts of fabric, and the office just stacked to the ceiling with papers. But some shops were really great, with laces and fabrics from France. Between that wonderful fabric, the board members' taste and the consignors' sewing skill and hard work…I worked closely with the consignors, and I loved it. There were ladies of every—I hate to say 'class'—every walk of life. I used to hate it when someone referred to our consignors as 'indigent.' I was not indigent. My husband had a heart attack and then was disabled. The best way it's ever been put is 'helping people help themselves.'"

Appendix B

Staff

Behind the Scenes

In 1982, Susan Rozmarin was unspooling bolts of raw silk, soft heavy tweed and crisp pique at Eunice Farmer Fabrics, teaching customers how to handle different textures. On display, along with the cubbyhole cylinders of jeweled and carved buttons, the mother-of-pearl belt buckles, the spools of striped grosgrain and plaid taffeta ribbon, hung baby dresses Rozmarin had smocked for Eunice Farmer's granddaughters. One afternoon, Rozmarin had expertly sheared a length of fabric for a customer and was neatly stacking her thread, pattern and bias tape on top of the folded yardage when Jacque Thieme walked in and started looking at the tiny dresses, peering at their elaborately worked bodices. Rozmarin thought maybe she was interested in taking one of the smocking classes. Oh, no. Thieme wanted Rozmarin to start sewing for the Exchange.

She agreed readily; she needed a new sewing machine, and with extra income, she could save for one. Early in 1998, she went to work on the selling floor of the Exchange. She sold children's clothes for five years and then began working directly with the consignors. Now she orders fabrics and laces for those who cannot afford them, keeping a ready stock of batiste, pique, pima cotton in tartan plaids, imperial broadcloth in pastels, seersucker, gingham, pinwale corduroy, velveteen and silk. She orders the fabric from Spechler-Vogel Textiles in New York and from a textile company in Alabama, and she buys double satin and grosgrain ribbon from Brewer

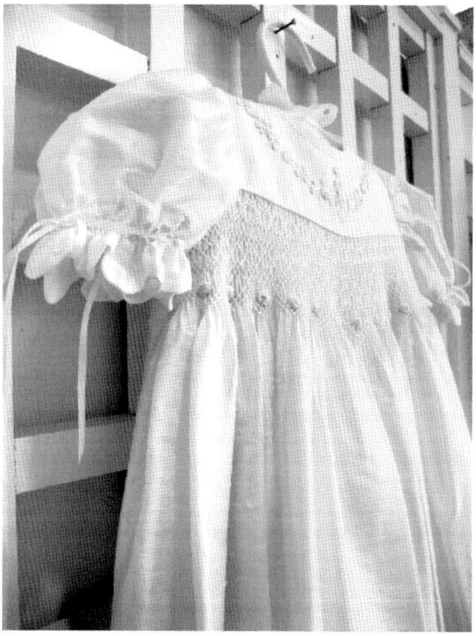

The Exchange's christening gowns are passed down for generations, initials embroidered at the hem for each new arrival.

Sewing Supplies. She makes sure to get French cotton lace, not the cheap, scratchy stuff, and the finest broadcloth, even when it's only for the handmade piping.

When a consignor has to be told her work is not up to Exchange standards, Rozmarin doesn't bear the burden alone. "We lay everything back on the board," she says with relief. "We have a committee who look at everything and approve it. Some things, I already know, just looking, that they're not the fabric we would use. And a lot of what we see is very craft show. If somebody makes something, though, they think it's beautiful, and it's difficult to turn them away."

She combs through magazines and catalogues for inspiration and then helps design patterns that skilled consignors can follow. Standards have loosened since she started—but only a little. "At first, everything had to be completely finished on the inside, with French seams and hand-stitched hems. Now," her voice lowers, "we let them use a serger for a blind hem."

At this writing, there are about 130 consignors, at their core a group of 10 who have worked steadily for the Exchange for decades. "Those who are very needy, we give them all the fabric, and they keep 70 to 90 percent of the selling price," Rozmarin says.

She still sews for her own pleasure, although she's stopped taking orders. "I learned to sew from my mom," she says. "I just love constructing something and seeing the finished product. I used to make christening gowns and flower girl dresses, and I loved to smock the infant things. There, you don't have to worry about size! Once you have to measure the girls and make sure the dresses fit, it gets difficult. Sometimes those flower girls have grown an inch between the fitting and the wedding!"

Invariably, she'd be working right up to the minute the garment was due. "Everything was hot off the press," she says, shaking her head, "and when you're just finishing up, sometimes you'll clip something you shouldn't and put a hole in it, and you just have to start over again. Every problem these consignors say they are having, I've had it."

Rozmarin smocked matching outfits for her three grandchildren on every holiday for eight or nine years. "One finally said, 'They're itchy, Granny!' They're not, they're just cotton, but the kids nowadays are used to knits. They don't really appreciate things that are dressier because they're so unused to wearing them."

Will the fine smocking end? She's not sure. "People don't know how to do it anymore," she sighs. They're still interested, though. The friend who took over her class still has a new crop of pupils every six weeks. "I also taught the French hand sewing, the beautiful, intricate lacework where you join laces together," Rozmarin says. "I've instructed people here—six women from Afghanistan. They were refugees and didn't speak English yet, so they had to have an interpreter. I taught them all to smock, but everybody except Zareen has stopped. They needed to be paid more. We paid twenty to twenty-five dollars to do just the panel, and it takes eight or nine hours. Then we'd have to pay someone to make the dress, and we couldn't price it too high."

Time costs money, and fine work is fast becoming unattainable.

In the Tearoom Kitchen

You can't talk about the kitchen of the Woman's Exchange without talking about Bertha Cook. She oversaw every dish for three decades, and she taught scores of cooks and waitresses and dishwashers what was what. "I would teach them to recognize authority and give them respect and be polite to the people," she says. "They all watched me, the ones who wanted to learn, and picked up what I did or didn't do."

Cook grew up working alongside her parents in the cotton fields of Carollton, Alabama. Her first food-prep job was for the Alabama Board of Education. "I did take classes to learn how to cook in large quantities, but I really learned at home, from my mom," she says. "She taught me everything to do to make it right." I ask what her mom made especially well, and she says, "Oh, Lord, everything she made was good. Her biscuits, I guess."

I tell Cook that everybody who worked for her talks about how wonderfully easygoing she was—yet what a high standard she set. "Well then," she says with a rich chuckle, "write what they told you."

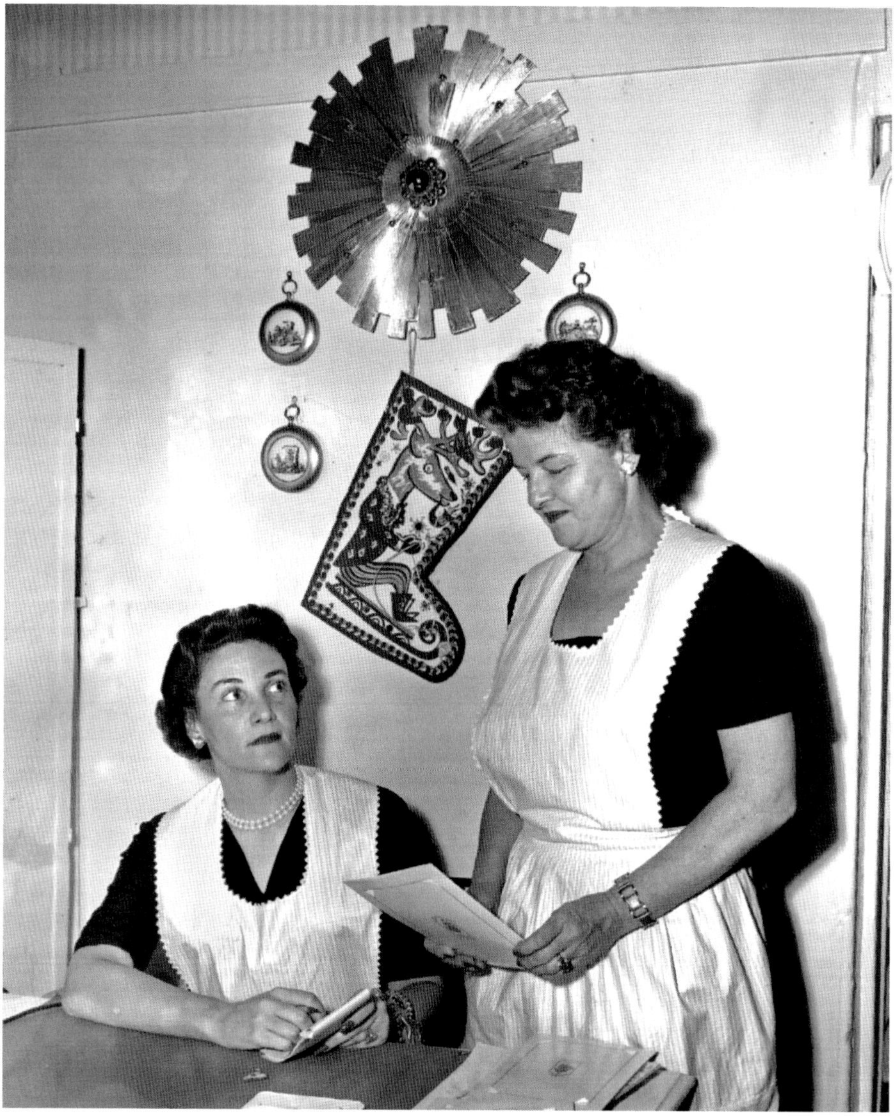

Service in the tearoom always had to be perfect. Ellie Schoenberg (left) concurs.

Surely something frustrated her, though? "Well, we had problems finding a dishwasher that was dedicated to the job," she drawls. "But we were a group that worked together. We all loved each other, and we'd just take turns and get it done."

I suddenly remember board member Edie Spink saying, "You've simply got to ask Bertha about ordering the chicken bosoms."

"Bosoms?" she repeats incredulously. Then she gives another long, low chuckle. "I don't think that was my language!" She remembers "the chicken man" well, but nothing about their interactions struck her as unusual. "Whenever I called him, he knew what I wanted, and he got it to me. If something didn't satisfy me, I'd just call and say, 'This won't work. Get me some fresher ones.'"

She told her staff the same thing. Melody Haffer, who now holds Cook's old job, remembers being constantly admonished to "rotate, rotate, rotate your stock, always keep it fresh. Don't serve anything you wouldn't want to eat."

Cook used to bake pies for the Exchange, and she grew famous for her fried chicken, even made it for board members' private parties. "There were a lot of things she did for the board on the side," remembers Haffer. "She would work at their houses, cater parties, cook them special things. Mrs. Eagleton liked tomato aspic, and Bertha would make it just for her."

There was a vast distance between the board members and many of the staff, in terms of background, worldview and values. But Cook says the work closed the gap, nearly always: "We got along woman to woman. I had respect for all of them."

Haffer, known as "Mel," has now worked for the Exchange one year longer than Cook did: thirty-one years. Haffer started there at sixteen, on the rebound from a disastrous high-school experience. "I had to switch from private to public, and it just was not the same—so I quit. My mother said, 'You cannot sit at home. If you're not going to school, you are going to work.' My sister was a manager at the Exchange back then. A salad girl position came open, and I went to work with my sister, and I've been here ever since.

"I was nervous and scared, but they welcomed me," she says. "Kids are totally different now, they've got their cellphones…I was just scared to death in the beginning. I wouldn't talk to anybody! I remember one time Helen, a waitress who was here forever, had taken out some hamburgers, and Bertha had set the buns on top of each other, and when she turned around with the burgers, Helen had already served the sandwiches! Just buns! Now we laugh, but we were always so worried about what the customers would think. We were conscientious.

"Back then, we had the cocktail bar," she adds, "but I was only sixteen. I was told not to even go over there." Instead, she did a lot of tedious labor—all the chopping, mincing and mixing for every chopped salad. "When I mixed the dressing I used the biggest pot we cook in, and made like two gallons at a time," she recalls. "Now, once a week, we make probably twenty-five or thirty gallons."

She's still making the same classics, like the Euclid Avenue sandwich, which used to be called the Exchange. "We mix mild and sharp cheddar—back in the day, we hand-grated all of that—with flour, milk, dry mustard and Worcestershire and crisscross bacon over the top. The cream cheese and olive is called the Maryland Avenue. I've been here so long, I can't even eat it anymore! I still like the coconut cake, though."

Dessert was the only part of her job that was cake. "We started getting too busy for ourselves, and I would get so stressed out," she remembers. "I was young, and I had orders coming from the front and the tearoom and carryout. But I had great help in the kitchen. Those ladies were just awesome. They took me under their wing and showed me how everything was done. I was pretty much raised here: Blanche [Roberts, one of the waitresses] is eighty now, and she still calls me her baby."

Haffer can make the Exchange's special salad dressing with her eyes shut, she says, "and we still hand chop the chicken and the celery. We tried once to run it through a chopper, and people noticed. I learned how to bone chicken from Bertha and how to make soups and stocks. I'd keep the spoon in so the soup wouldn't stick to the bottom, because that's what she said, and I used to listen to everything she said.

"I learned a lot from my mom, too, because she was from the South," Haffer adds. "The beef vegetable soup on the menu was her recipe. I was really nervous about it, because it's a time-consuming soup to make, but everybody said, 'We can do it.'" Over the years, Haffer gained confidence, until she was running the kitchen, creating new specials and concocting entrées for the 125th anniversary.

But she still trembles when the electricity flickers.

"We used to have power outages where we'd lose all refrigeration," she explains, "and everybody would have to quick take things home to put in their own freezers." There was the occasional plumbing problem, too—she remembers sweeping great swooshes of water out the back door one day. "And anything bad to clean up, like raw eggs or dressing, I've dropped it! I knocked the butter pot off the stove once—it spun and just flipped right off the stove, and the butter for the grilled cheeses went everywhere."

No matter what happened, they all pitched in, scrubbed the kitchen back to immaculate, pulled the orders together so they'd taste just as good as the last time. For waitress Nina Reilly, a good day is the tearoom packed with customers, ordering "lots of different things—and dessert. What I tell my new customers is, 'If you've never been here, you need to share our house salad and our signature sandwich, and then split a piece of pie.

"Our salads are huge; we're known for that," she adds proudly. "The Euclid is a piece and a half of bread, covered in a rich cheese mixture—we don't tell people too much what goes in our stuff, 'cause it's kind of like a secret. We broil the cheese and top it with crispy bacon. The cream cheese and olive is the Maryland Avenue; that one's an old recipe. People who like it *really* like it, and you can't get it anywhere else. But I don't think we've ever had a young person order it! Now we have wraps, and that's what the younger crowd's ordering. Our hummus wrap is really good, with fresh radishes and carrots. Our soups are fantastic, especially our vegetable beef on Wednesday, our baked potato soup on Fridays. And people love our shrimp special on Fridays." And then, of course, there's the famous lemon meringue pie, the coconut crème pie, the chocolate-mint brownie…

"This," says Reilly, "is a pretty cool little job."

At the Helm

Jessica Wright became executive director of the Exchange in 2005, at one of those make-or-break moments. The Exchange was pulling itself out of a financial crisis and reeling from two years without a manager.

"I saw the ad in the paper," she recalls. "I'd always done a lot of nonprofit volunteer work, and I had a background in retail." After studying hard and immersing herself in extracurricular activities all through high school, Wright had gone off to Vassar University—and hated it. "Which was quite a shock. I came home, and for the first time, I didn't have this structured life. I decided to get a job and then start over in the fall somewhere else." Instead, she fell in love with the world of work: the interaction with people, the merchandising, the problem solving, figuring out what you have that meets someone's needs.

When she interviewed for the job at the Exchange, Tara Lewis clued her in pretty bluntly about the financial challenges. She wasn't fazed.

"Everything crashed after 9/11, so financial difficulties were not unusual," Wright says. "I'd already worked at two companies that hadn't survived, so I kind of understood what it was to manage through a financial crisis. And I could tell they hadn't put a lot of things in place that people use to run a business." Like a budget—for years, they'd navigated without one. And computerized inventory—they weren't breaking it down by sizes, so they

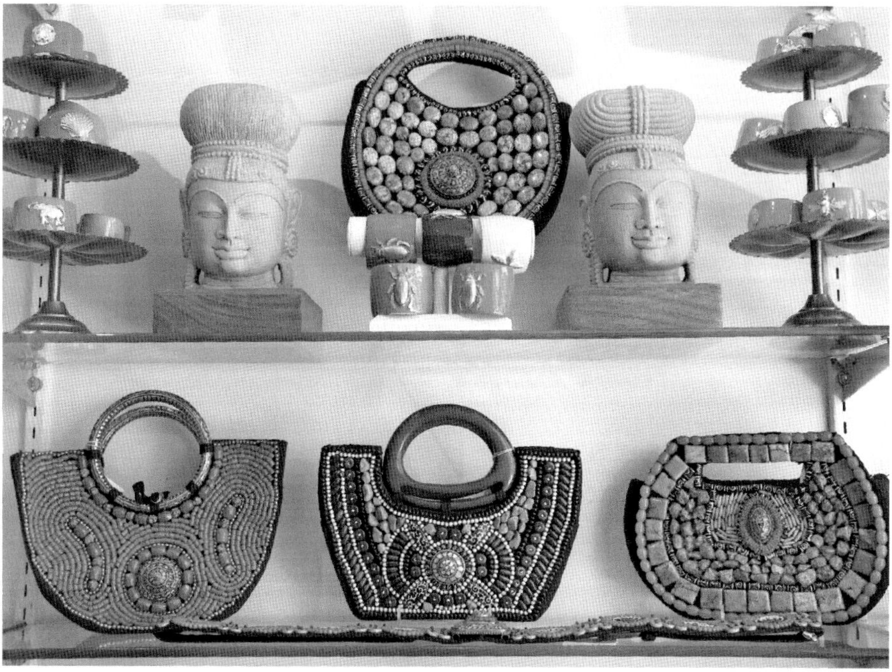

Purses have come a long way from the patent-leather clutch.

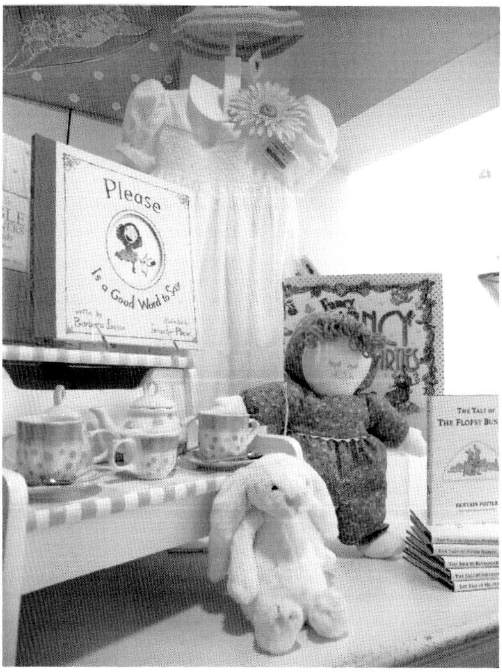

A holiday display pulls together hand-smocked dresses, hand-sewn dolls, hand-painted toys and bought-outright bunnies.

didn't know what was selling out. She started using more quantitative data, reshaping systems to get the kind information on the front end that she'd need to measure results and plan for the future. She taught the staff to use technology more fully and more efficiently.

And they taught her to slow down.

"My biggest lesson here has been to be conservative in the changes that take place," she admits. "I am someone who thinks constantly, 'How can we change this to make it better?'—and the reality is that people don't want a lot of change. If we change so much as the brand of bacon, some will like it and others won't, and we will hear about it for months. People want everything on the menu exactly the same way it was. They do not want the recipes to change. They do not want a lighter version of the salad."

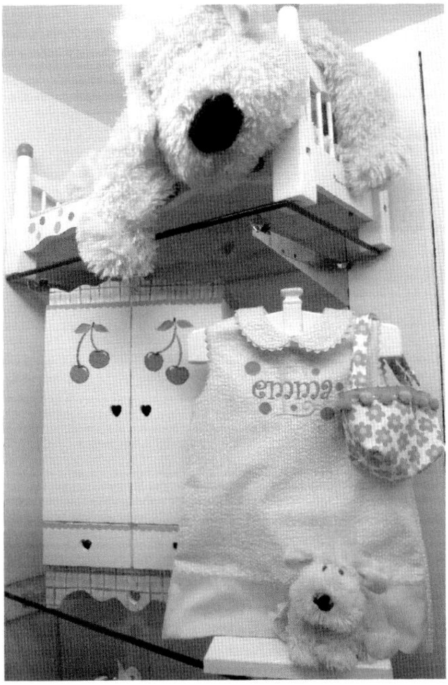

The preppie pink and spring green combination will never go away.

Clothes aren't much easier. "We try to change just one thing at a time," Wright says. "If it's a totally different silhouette, we will try to do it in a color our customers are used to seeing and vice versa. That way, it kind of fits into the shop." Color's been cast in stone for quite some time. Consignors talk about "the Woman's Exchange colors" and sigh regretfully over the pale greens, purples and oranges that just won't fly.

"Well, we've been trying to bring a little bit in," Wright mock-whispers. "Every once in a while, a purple hair bow. And brown stuffed animals. I remember looking at an adorable little stuffed brown dog we could sell, and someone said, 'Oh, we don't do brown.' I said, 'But dogs are brown! Bears, too.' They said, 'We don't do brown. We don't do brown.' Well, we do now. Our plush reps are so excited, they don't know what to do with themselves!"

Wright's had great fun bringing in the latest accessories, from chunky wooden jewelry and native beads to scarves imported from Mexico, high-style contemporary glassware and serving pieces and intensely colored purses.

There's nothing pastel about the spirit of today's Exchange.

Bibliography

Bushle, Mari Jo. "Needlewomen and the Vicissitudes of Modern Life: A Study of Middle-Class Construction in the Antebellum Northeast." In *Visible Women: New Essays on American Activism*. Edited by Nancy A. Hewitt and Suzanne Lebsock. Urbana: University of Illinois Press, 1993.

Corbett, Katharine T., and Howard S. Miller. *Saint Louis in the Gilded Age*. St. Louis: Missouri Historical Society Press, 1993.

Crawford, Louis Lawnin. "A Brief History of the Nelson-Lawnin-Crawford-Bevis Families." Unpublished ms., December 1984.

De Tocqueville, Alexis, Richard C. Heffner and Vartan Gregorian. *Democracy in America*. New York: Penguin, 2010.

Katz, Michael B. *In the Shadow of the Poorhouse: A Social History of Welfare in America*. New York: Basic Books, 1986.

Lincoln, F.A. *Directory of Exchanges for Woman's Work: With Methods for Dealing with Them*. Springfield, MA: F.A. Lincoln, 1891.

Missouri Department of Labor and Industrial Inspection. *1891 Annual Report*. Bureau of Labor Statistics, 1891.

Missouri Republican, 1883.

Philadelphia Ladies Depository. *Annual Report of the Managers of the Ladies Depository*. Library Company of Philadelphia, 1834.

Rybczynski, Witold. *Home: A Short History of an Idea*. New York: Viking, 1986.

Sander, Kathleen Waters. *The Business of Charity: The Woman's Exchange Movement, 1832–1900*. Urbana: University of Illinois Press, 1998.

St. Louis Globe-Democrat, 1883–1986.

St. Louis Post-Dispatch, 1882–2008.

Thelen, David Paul. *Paths of Resistance: Tradition and Dignity in Industrializing Missouri*. New York: Oxford University Press, 1986.

Trebay, Guy. "In an Easter Dress, a Social Set Revealed." *New York Times*, March 18, 2007.

Whitaker, Jan. *Tea at the Blue Lantern Inn: A Social History of the Tea Room Craze in America*. New York: St. Martin's Press, 2002.

Woman's Exchange of St. Louis. Minutes of the Annual and Executive Meetings, 1883–2008. Along with correspondence, photographs, newsletters and ephemera.

Index

A

Alcott, Louisa May 15
Allen, Sarah W. 38
Armory Fête 17

B

Baer, J. Arthur "Cubby" 73
Bailey, Helen 130
Bakelite 38
Baker, Al 67
Banister, F.A. 41, 42
Barlow, John 67
Barr, William 35
Baur, Shellie 86, 99, 112
Bean, Sharon 45, 100, 101, 107, 108, 123
Big Cinch 60
Branca, Alessandra 125
Brandin, Pitti 77, 90
Brown v. Board of Education 65
Busch, Lilly Eberhard Anheuser 30

C

Cady, Lisa 122, 123
California pottery 60, 62
Cella, Charles 74, 77, 100, 105, 107, 116
Cella, Louis 100
Chalfant, Sue 58, 75, 78, 79, 81, 84
Chandler, Dian (now Dian Shock) 52
Chandler, Tudie 52, 53, 67
Charles P. Chouteau 18
Chouteau, Pierre 20
Cincinnati Exchange 63
Condie, Lamie 96
Condie, Lamy 73
Cook, Bertha 83, 93, 108, 117, 147–150
Cornwell, Mary 77, 83
Cozadd, Rita 131, 132
Craft, Kathey 129, 130, 131
Crawford, Ginny 77
Creve Coeur Lake 16, 17
Crinoline Bar, New York Exchange for Woman's Work 51
Culver, Jane 47, 73, 75, 96

D

Dacey, Corinne 104
Dames, Joan 99
Degenhart, Patricia 133
Desloge, Mrs. Theodore 65
Dobler, Irene 46, 50, 51, 53, 56–58, 65
dress code 108
Dressel, Ellie 97, 98, 127–129
Drey, Barbar Blair 66
Duffy, Robert 75

E

Eagleton, Elaine 69, 73, 96, 149
Edward L. Bakewell Real Estate Co. 48
Ellie Shoenberg 70
English muffins 93, 94, 117
Ephron, Nora 96

F

Fort, Mary 100, 102
Fouke, Becky 81
Fouke, Claude 68
Fusz, Mrs. Louis Jr. 94

G

Galt, Marianne 67, 90, 91, 93, 94, 96, 98, 99
Gardner, Carol Moon "Moody" 52
Gardner, Margaret 67
Garrett, Gayle 107
Good Housekeeping 39
Gordon, Julia Lawnin 52, 73
Gourmet magazine 102

H

Haffer, Melody 117, 149, 150
Hargadine McKittrick Dry Goods Co. 35
Heilman, Jill 103
Heim, Violette 52, 53, 85, 87, 93, 95, 97, 98
Hoerr, Kelly 118
Holmes, Irene 67–70, 92
Homer, Mrs. W.B. 31
Honig, Larry 110
Howe, Julia Ward 15
Hummert, Hilda 79

J

Junior League 45

K

Katy Lou Wade 53
Katzman, Diane 117
Katzman, Susan 104
Kaufman, Chris 105
Kennedy, Jacqueline 125, 127
Korean War 61, 62
koumiss tonic 26

L

Lawnin, Albert 17
Lawnin, Ariadne Worthington 16–18, 20, 21, 23–26, 31, 37–39, 73, 94
Lawnin, Joseph DeMontalte 16, 17, 20, 39
Lawnin, Louis 17, 39
Levis, Sophie 67
Lewis, Tara 112–114, 122, 124, 151
Long, Mrs. E.H. 32, 34

M

Martin, Julia Gordon 52
Matthews, Kary 102, 109, 110, 121, 123, 124
Matthews, Muffy 80
May Company 80, 110
McAlpin, Anne Stupp 66, 67, 76, 100, 106
McClellan, Bill 107
McReynolds, Jess 52, 68, 98
Montileone, Ralph 66
Morgan, Eliza 31

N

National Federation of Woman's Exchanges 45, 57, 93, 95, 98, 101, 102, 123
Nelson, N.O. 22
New York Exchange for Woman's Work 16, 42, 51
Nina Reilly 150

O

Orthwein, Tillie 30, 116

P

Paltrow, Gwyneth 125, 127
Pantaleoni, Jane 101
Pappagallo's 84, 107
Perry, Mrs. William D. 74
Peters, Cynthia 78
Petersmeyer, Linda 117, 135, 136
Philadelphia Ladies' Depository 14, 15
Pickwick Theater 17, 20, 22
Pinkerton detectives 61
Pollnow, Lissy 105
Price, Vincent 125
psycograph 45

R

Rand, Mary Frances 58
Razawi, Zareen 139, 141
Reed, Diane 103
Reilly, Nina 150, 151
Rich, Frieda 103
Robert, Mrs. P.G. 37
Roberts, Barbara 71, 88, 89, 142
Rogers, Penny 88, 89, 99, 142
Roos, Mrs. Lawrence K. 94
Rosen, Betty 69, 77
Rouse, Hope Jones 106
Rouse, Janey 81, 92, 100, 106, 112, 121, 141
Rozmarin, Susan 140, 145–147

S

Sanquinette, Mabs 79
Schnuck, Lucy 101, 102
Schrick, Carol 89, 134
Schroer, Pauline 138, 139
Scott, Ann 91, 97, 98, 99, 124
Selkirk, Laurie (Mrs. Bruce) 88, 94, 97, 141, 142
Senturia, Nancy 56, 57
Sexton, Lottie (Mrs. L.F.) 40
Sherman, William Tecumseh 27
Shoenberg, Ellie 70, 72, 73, 78, 84, 96
Simmons, E.C. 33
Spechler-Vogel Textiles 85, 145
Spink, Edie 50, 77, 78, 81–84, 86, 87, 121, 148
Stix, Baer & Fuller 42, 73
Stott, Elizabeth 13, 14, 15
suffrage 39

T

Talent, U.S. representative James 102
Thieme, Jacque 81, 85–87, 90, 91, 93–95, 99–103, 107, 108, 112, 113, 131, 136, 141, 142, 145
Thrasher, Brenda 136–138
Torre, Joe 121
Town & Country 63, 95

V

Vandervoort's 42, 54, 57
Volkman, Janet 73, 96

W

Wade, Katy Lou 53, 54, 56, 60
Wagner, Maureen 133
Wells, David 71, 90
Women's Christian Association 16, 18
World War II 59
Worthington, Ariadne. *See* Lawnin, Ariadne Worthington
Worthington, Elizabeth Sappington 16
Wright, Jessica 114, 115, 118–120, 151, 153

Y

Yoder, Susie 93

About the Author

Jeannette Batz Cooperman has long been fascinated by the domestic arts—in theory if not in practice. She holds a doctorate in American studies from Saint Louis University, and her dissertation, published as *The Broom Closet*, focused on domestic ritual in post-feminist literature. Her undergraduate degrees were in philosophy and communication. Currently a staff writer for *St. Louis Magazine*, she has been accepted into the American Society of Journalists and Authors, and she has won national awards for her narrative journalism and investigative reporting. This is her fifth book.